Teacher's Guide
Set 4 Discoveries

Modern Curriculum Press

DISCOVERIES: SET 4

CONTENTS

TEACHER'S GUIDE

Program Overview	3
Scope & Sequence	6
Ongoing Assessment	7
Observation Checklist	8
About the Theme: Discoveries	9
Project Ideas	10
Bibliography	11

Discovering the Titanic — 12
- Before Reading — 14
- During Reading — 17
- After Reading — 20
- Skill Mini-Lessons — 21
- Home-School Master — 24
- Skill Masters — 25

Through the Garden Door — 28
- Before Reading — 30
- During Reading — 33
- After Reading — 36
- Skill Mini-Lessons — 37
- Home-School Master — 40
- Skill Masters — 41

On the Way to the Moon — 44
- Before Reading — 46
- During Reading — 49
- After Reading — 52
- Skill Mini-Lessons — 53
- Home-School Master — 56
- Skill Masters — 57

The Lost and Found Game — 60
- Before Reading — 62
- During Reading — 65
- After Reading — 68
- Skill Mini-Lessons — 69
- Home-School Master — 72
- Skill Masters — 73

Secrets of the Rain Forest — 76
- Before Reading — 78
- During Reading — 81
- After Reading — 84
- Skill Mini-Lessons — 85
- Home-School Master — 88
- Skill Masters — 89

Strategic Reading Masters — 92
Index

Program Overview

" My students are always asking to read books that look more grown-up than picture books. But they're not quite ready for long novels and nonfiction books. What can I give them? "

" Many of my students want to read books and stories about topics and themes that are related to our curriculum. Where can I find books that I know they'll be able to read? "

If you've often asked yourself similar questions, *MCP Early Chapter Books* is the program for you. *MCP Early Chapter Books* is a unique program of 60 books on three levels specially designed to form a bridge between picture books and full-length novels and works of nonfiction. *Very First Chapters* is aimed at fluent readers who are reading at the first–second grade level. *First Chapters* is meant for readers at the second–third grade level. *Next Chapters* is appropriate for on-level third–fourth grade readers and reluctant older readers. *MCP Early Chapter Books* is one of the only programs to blend quality reading experiences for your students with a flexible teaching plan that provides plenty of skills development to address a variety of learning styles, activities, and opportunities to assess students' progress.

This complete teaching plan also includes several reproducible pages for all 60 books in the program. **You** will love having the option of two instructional paths—one for students who can use the books independently and one for students who need more direct instructional support. Your **students** will love the more sophisticated look and feel of a first novel or nonfiction book, with a comfortable reading level of 1.6–2.3 for *Very First Chapters*, a reading level of 2.4–3.1 for *First Chapters*, and a reading level of 3.2–3.9 for *Next Chapters*.

First Chapters Components

Each of the 20 chapter books in *First Chapters* is a book your students will love. Engrossing and engaging stories and subjects along with high-quality illustrations and photographs make these books your students will want to read again and again. A complete teaching plan has been designed for each book so that you can teach before, during, and after your students read with activities that address multiple intelligences, prior knowledge activities, Internet activities, and comprehension, study skills, vocabulary, word study, and strategic reading instruction.

Set 4 DISCOVERIES

20 Interesting and Engaging Chapter Books

The books are specifically aimed at fluent readers who are ready for early chapter books.

- The 20 books are divided into 4 sets of 5 books each. Each set fits a theme so that readers can make thematic connections among several texts, while exploring different aspects of the theme.
- Second–third grade reading range allows for children of a variety of reading levels to read the books independently or with teacher support.
- Each set is comprised of fiction and nonfiction in a variety of genres to offer a wide range of reading experiences.
- There is just the right balance of text and photos or illustrations to engage students' interest and to support their reading.
- Fiction titles are 64 pages, nonfiction titles are 48 pages—longer than picture books, shorter than full-length novels and nonfiction books—the right length to support developing readers.
- There is a glossary and a table of contents in every book, and an index in all of the nonfiction titles to provide students with the experience of using a variety of standard book features and resources.
- One fiction book in each of the four sets contains the same characters, the Quincy Kids, which provides opportunities for making connections among several texts and for understanding and enjoying the characters.

Nature	You and Your Community	Creative Solutions	Discoveries
1 *Animal Champions* by Teri Crawford Jones RL 3.0	**6** *Let's Build a Playground* by Edward Myers RL 2.9	**11** *Whoops! It Works!* by Orlando Lopez RL 3.1	**16** *Discovering the Titanic* by Cindy Trumbore RL 3.0
2 *Quackers, the Troublesome Duck** by Leslie Ellen RL 2.5	**7** *A Day at the Races* by Eric Michaels RL 2.6	**12** *How Bullfrog Found His Sound* by Eric Michaels RL 2.6	**17** *Through the Garden Door* by Barbara Reeves RL 2.4
3 *Digging Dinosaurs* by Judy Nayer RL 2.7	**8** *Best Wishes for Eddie** by Judy Nayer RL 2.4	**13** *Living in Space* by Judy Nayer RL 3.0	**18** *On the Way to the Moon* by Becky Gold RL 3.1
4 *The Day the Sky Turned Green* by Barbara Reeves RL 2.5	**9** *New Year's Around the World* by Cindy Trumbore RL 2.9	**14** *Making Lily Laugh* by Ellen Dreyer RL 2.5	**19** *The Lost and Found Game** by Judy Nayer RL 2.5
5 *Chasing Tornadoes* by Becky Gold RL 2.9	**10** *Starfishers to the Rescue* by Ellen Dreyer RL 2.7	**15** *The Great Riddle Mystery** by James R. MacLean RL 2.6	**20** *Secrets of the Rain Forest* by Edward Myers RL 3.1

 =nonfiction   *=Books that feature the Quincy Kids   RL=Reading Level

Set 4 DISCOVERIES

Teacher's Guides
One comprehensive guide per set of chapter books

Each Teacher's Guide offers a variety of activities, skill mini-lessons, and teaching ideas to enhance students' development of reading and language arts skills and strategies.

• A **teaching plan** for each book in a set focuses on Before Reading, During Reading, and After Reading so that you have a wide array of skills, and activities to choose from as students approach, read, and complete each book.

• Strategies for a range of different learning styles include activities that address **Multiple Intelligences** and **English as a Second Language** so that you can easily customize instruction.

• **Two different instructional paths** — one for students who are reading independently and one for students who need more teacher support — give you greater flexibility in managing and customizing instructional time.

• **Critical thinking and reader response** questions are provided on a chapter-by-chapter basis for students who need greater instructional support, and at the midpoint and end of the book for students who are reading independently. Teachable Moments enable you to teach skills, using models and examples from the stories, at the point at which students encounter them.

• **Six Skill Mini-Lessons** and a strategic reading lesson that address comprehension, study skills, word study, vocabulary, and strategic reading skills are included in each lesson plan.

• **A Home-School Connection** in each teaching plan in English and Spanish involves families in your students' learning.

• **Cross-curricular activities**, including Internet activities, provide additional support for other areas of your curriculum and enhance themes you are using in your classroom.

Using *First Chapters*
How can I adapt *First Chapters* to my classroom needs?

With two teaching options provided in every plan, you can customize instruction for all of the students in your class.

• If individuals or groups of students can read for sustained periods and do not need skills support as they read, choose the **Independent Reading** teaching path.

• If you feel that individuals or groups would benefit from the added instructional support of chapter-by-chapter comprehension checks and skills teaching, select the **Teacher Supported Reading** teaching path in the plan.

Where does *First Chapters* fit in if I'm using a basal program?

First Chapters was designed to work hand in hand with any basal reading program. The books in *First Chapters* offer additional reading support for common basal themes.

• *First Chapters* offers skills support for the most important comprehension, study skills, word study, and strategic reading skills.

• Six Skill Mini-Lessons are included in every teaching plan along with a strategy for interactive reading.

• Included are reproducible Skill Masters tailored to every lesson and five strategy masters that can be used with any book in the program or any basal reading selection.

How will my students use the books?

• *First Chapters* provides the flexibility of a library book program with the distinction of including a complete Teacher's Guide to enhance students' reading experience.

• You can invite students to select the books they are most interested in reading.

• If your students are studying a specific topic, you can choose when your students read a particular book.

• You can elect to have small groups in your class read different books that relate to the same theme in a set.

Set 4 DISCOVERIES

Scope & Sequence

BOOK	1	2	3	4	5	6	7	8	9	10	11	12	13	14	15	16	17	18	19	20
COMPREHENSION																				
Author's craft														•			•			
Author's purpose			•																•	
Cause/effect relationships					•		•						•			•				
Character		•						•							•				•	
Classifying	•										•							•		
Dialogue								•												
Drawing conclusions			•																	•
Fact/fantasy											•									
Humor														•						
Idioms														•						
Imagery																	•			
Main idea and details	•					•					•									•
Making comparisons	•									•			•							
Making inferences				•											•					
Making judgments						•			•						•					
Making predictions		•															•			
Paraphrasing											•							•		
Plot							•													
Point of view				•															•	
Referents				•																
Sequence			•				•													
Setting										•	•									
Theme										•	•									
Types of literature					•					•					•					
WORD STUDY																				
Analogies										•	•						•			
Comparatives	•												•							
Compound words		•			•						•								•	
Context clues					•				•							•				
Contractions		•						•												
Homophones/Homographs								•				•		•						
Inflected forms				•										•			•			
Multiple-meaning words								•			•									•
Plurals						•									•					
Possessives			•										•							
Prefixes											•							•		
Specialized vocabulary												•								•
Suffixes	•				•												•			
Syllabication			•		•															
Synonyms/Antonyms				•						•			•							
STUDY SKILLS																				
Using alphabetical order		•												•	•					
Using a dictionary			•								•									
Using an encyclopedia				•						•										
Following directions							•								•		•			
Locating sources of information						•						•					•			
SQ3R																				•
Using standard book features										•	•					•				
Taking notes						•														
Test-taking strategies					•								•							
Using graphic aids	•	•		•		•												•		
Using resources										•		•							•	•
STRATEGIC READING																				
Adjusting reading rate, reading ahead, rereading						•									•					
Organizing information						•														
Confirming predictions		•																		
Problem/Solution														•						
Self-assess																		•		
Self-questioning	•						•						•							
Summarizing			•						•											
Synthesizung																				•
Using picture clues													•							
Using prior knowledge										•	•									
Visualizing				•			•					•			•		•	•	•	

Set 4 DISCOVERIES

Ongoing Assessment

First Chapters provides many opportunities for you to gather information about how your students are developing as readers. Monitoring how students participate in partner, small group, or whole class activities in conjunction with individual conferences can provide the information you need to evaluate students' progress.

Each teaching plan in *First Chapters* is designed so you can easily evaluate how well your students are understanding what they read. Use the **Comprehension Check** questions as well as the **Reader Response** questions to gain insight about your students' comprehension of every book.

The Skill Mini-Lessons provide opportunities to assess how well your students are learning comprehension, study skills, and word study skills. The **Evaluate** section of each Skill Mini-Lesson provides an opportunity to assess how well students are acquiring skills. Observe how your students apply these skills as they read further in each chapter book, as they read additional chapter books, and as they read other material.

Observation

"Kidwatching" is an activity that most teachers do naturally and provides a wealth of information about how well students are learning. There are several ways to organize the data that observing your students yields.

Anecdotal records are one way to take a short, written snapshot of the behaviors you observe. You can keep your records in notebooks or on index cards.

> Friday, October 28
> Rosa conducted an interview as part of a Reader Response activity after she read *Digging Dinosaurs*. As she introduced herself as a Tyrannosaurus rex, she recalled several of the physical characteristics of this meat-eating dinosaur.

Checklists are another useful way to keep written records, since observable behaviors are identified. An observation checklist has been included in the *First Chapters* Teacher's Guide on page 8. Use it to record data about your students' progress with reading skills, strategies, and behaviors.

Portfolios are another good way to evaluate students' progress over time. Many of the end products of activities in the *First Chapters* teaching plans can be added to students' portfolios.

Look for the portfolio icon next to activities under **Support All Learners, Addressing Multiple Intelligences, Reader Response Activities,** and **Curriculum Connections.** This icon signifies that the end products of particular activities might make good additions to students' portfolios.

There are three **Skill Masters** at the end of each teaching plan. Any or all of these masters can also be placed in students' portfolios. In addition to the Skill Masters, there are five graphic organizers for **Strategic Reading** at the end of every Teacher's Guide. Completed Strategic Reading Masters might also make good portfolio pieces.

Set 4 DISCOVERIES

Observation Checklist

Reading Strategies	Beginning	Developing	Skilled
Relies on print more than illustrations			
Can predict words using visual cues			
Makes comparisons between similar words			
Understands punctuation			
Can sustain silent reading			
Can self-correct			
Comprehension			
Can make and confirm predictions			
Can predict outcomes			
Can read for meaning			
Identifies sequence of events			
Can retell a story			
Summarizes			
Can relate main idea			
Can use literature as a springboard for creative responses			
Can apply what is read to new situations			
Makes judgments about reading material			
Evaluates and applies what is learned			
Reading Behaviors			
Enjoys reading			
Contributes to discussions			
Reads independently			
Is an expressive reader			

ABOUT THE THEME: Discoveries

To make a discovery is to find out something previously unknown. That is why making discoveries can be so exciting. Sometimes people spend their entire lives hoping to make a discovery—to find something no one else has found.

Discoveries is the theme of Set 4 of *First Chapters*. Each of the five books in the set centers around discoveries—a sunken ship, a fantastic garden, the moon, a game, and the rain forest.

Discovering the Titanic is the story of one of the greatest discoveries of the twentieth century. The book tells about the famous ocean liner and the fateful night of April 14, 1912, when the colossal ship struck an iceberg and sank.

Reading Level 3.0

Through the Garden Door is a fantasy about two children, who follow a strange creature through a doorway and find themselves in a very unusual garden.

Reading Level 2.4

On the Way to the Moon focuses on the discoveries people have made about the moon—from what Galileo learned about the Moon's surface 400 years ago to the recent discovery of ice on the moon.

Reading Level 3.1

In *The Lost and Found Game*, the Quincy Kids hold a rummage sale to raise money for new baseball uniforms. Among the things given to them by Jody's grandfather, they discover a mysterious box. It turns out to be an old Wari board, an ancient game from Africa. The kids decide to make and sell their own Wari boards, which earns them enough money to buy uniforms for the whole team.

Reading Level 2.5

Secrets of the Rain Forest takes readers to one of Earth's most amazing ecosystems—tropical rain forests. Here live animals and plants that are not found anywhere else on the planet. The wonders of the rain forest are explored along with an explanation of why rain forests are so valuable.

Reading Level 3.1

Besides presenting fascinating information about discoveries and exciting, fun stories of discovery, the books also relate to each other. For example, students will read about one scientist who discovered the wreck of the *Titanic* in *Discovering the Titanic*, then read about all the discoveries made by astronauts and other scientists in *On the Way to the Moon*. After reading about two children who discover a beautiful garden in *Through the Garden Door*, students will read about the natural treasures found in rain forests. In *Secrets of the Rain Forest*, students learn that rain forests have existed for thousands of years, while in *The Lost and Found Game* they learn about a game that is more than 3,000 years old.

Set 4 DISCOVERIES

PROJECT IDEAS

To help students learn more about discoveries and make some discoveries of their own, you may wish to use any of the following project ideas for the Discoveries theme.

Discovering New Places

Objective: To help students discover new and unusual places, have them create and record their own investigations.
Materials: art materials; reference materials; maps or a globe

Organizing the Project
Prewriting

Separate the class into three or four groups. Invite each group to decide if they want to visit an imaginary place, like the garden in *Through the Garden Door*, a far-away place somewhere in the world, or a place that is even further away, like the moon. Provide reference materials to help groups with ideas. Encourage students to think of or find out as much information as they can about their place. Then, within each group, have each student choose one of the following roles:

- **Mapping:** Decide where your place is. Then think about how you would get there.
- **Drawing:** Find out or decide what you would see in your place.
- **Writing:** Tell about your place. What would you see, hear, smell, taste, or touch? How hot or cold, wet or dry is it? Who might you meet? How would you travel around in this place? What might you discover?
- **Making Models:** Think about what things, people, or creatures you might discover or meet in your place. What would they look like?

Drafting

Have groups discuss how they want to present the information they have collected. For example:

- **Mapping:** Draw a map that shows the route to take from your classroom or community to your place. Write what kind of transportation you would use.
- **Drawing:** Draw pictures or collect photographs from old magazines.
- **Writing:** Write a description of your place. Tell about the land and any people or animals that live there.
- **Making Models:** Make models of any things, people, and/or creatures in your place. Create a diorama by putting your models together with the pictures drawn or collected by the Drawing group.

Responding/Revising/Proofreading

Allow groups time to look over their writing to check for complete sentences, descriptive words, spelling, and punctuation.

Publishing the Project

You may wish to display projects in the classroom. Encourage the different groups to present their projects. Then invite the rest of the class to act as explorers and tour the places created by each group.

Planning a Scavenger Hunt

Objective: To help students enjoy the fun of discovery, organize a class scavenger hunt.
Materials: items to hide

Organizing the Project

Divide the class into four or more groups. Invite each group to plan several "treasures," such as a book or a small wooden box with a coin or other object inside, that can be hidden around the classroom, or, if possible, around the school. Then have each group decide where they will hide their treasures and write clues to find each one.

If you are able to have the scavenger hunt beyond the classroom, arrange a day. Also set aside time when each group can hide their treasures in the planned places. Then have groups exchange clues. You may wish

Set 4 DISCOVERIES

to have all of the groups start at the same time, or have groups hunt one at a time. Limit the hunt to 15 or 20 minutes, cautioning students not to run.

Publishing the Project

After the hunt is over, call on each group to display the items they were able to find. If any items were not found, ask the group who wrote the clues to tell what and where the item is.

Researching Discoveries

Objective: To help students understand the importance of discoveries in the world today, have them keep track of information about discoveries.

Materials: current newspapers and news magazines; access to the Internet (optional)

Organizing the Project

Explain to students that discoveries are being made every day, especially in the field of medicine and other sciences. You may wish to give an example of the recent discovery of ice on the moon.

Have students form small groups of four. Encourage each group to look through current newspapers, news magazines, or watch news broadcasts or appropriate documentaries to learn more about a recent discovery in medicine, outer space, ancient civilizations, or other fields. If you have access to Internet research, you may want to add it as a possible resource. Provide guidance as necessary to help each group choose one item to report on.

Publishing the Project

Have each group write a one-page summary about the discovery they found. Then have them present their findings to the class.

For Students

Bess, Clayton. *The Truth About the Moon.* Houghton Mifflin, 1983.

Brewster, Hugh and Laurie Coulter. *888 ½ Amazing Answers to Questions About the Titanic.* Scholastic Trade, 1998.

Chandler, Clare. *Little Green Fingers: A Kid's Guide to Growing Things.* Whitecap Books, 1996.

Donnelly, Judy. *True-Life Treasure Hunts.* Random House, 1993.

Kusugak, Michael. *Hide and Sneak.* Annick Press, 1992.

McGuire, J. Victor. *Takiya and Thunderheart's Life Garden.* Spice of Life Educational Publishing, 1997.

Simon, Seymour. *The Moon.* Macmillan, 1984.

Yorinks, Arthur. *Company's Coming.* Crown, 1992.

For Parents and Teachers

Ballard, Dr. Robert. *The Discovery of the Titanic.* Warner, 1995.

Goodman, Billy. *The Rainforest.* Tern Enterprise, 1991.

Hamilton, Jean. *Tropical Rainforests.* Silver Burdett Press, 1995.

Marsh, Ed W. *James Cameron's Titanic.* HarperCollins, 1997.

Powell, Darlene, Derek S. Hopson, and Tom Clavin. *Juba This and Juba That: 100 African-American Games for Children.* Simon & Schuster, 1996.

Time-Life Books (editors). *Moons and Rings, Voyage Through the Universe.* Time-Life Books, 1991.

DISCOVERIES: BOOK 16

DISCOVERING THE TITANIC

GENRE: NONFICTION

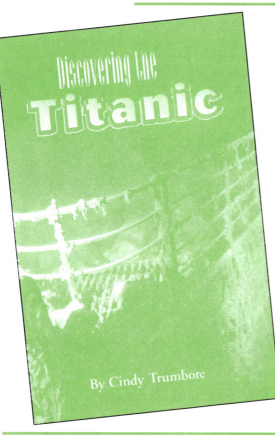

Summary

Discovering the Titanic explores the famous ocean liner and tells the story of the fateful night of April 14–15, 1912 when the ship struck an iceberg and sank. Of the more than 2,000 people aboard the *Titanic*, only about 700 survived. The book describes the attempts made to discover the wreck, and the various inventions that were developed to aid the search. Finally, in 1985, Dr. Robert Ballard of the Woods Hole Oceanographic Institution, was successful in locating the *Titanic*. With the help of underwater robots, he was able to film the wreck and solve several mysteries. The book ends with a description of the filming of James Cameron's 1997 motion picture, *Titanic*.

ome-School Connection

The Home-School activity master on page 24 of this Teacher's Guide provides a variety of activities students can do at home with family members.

PLANNER

SKILLS OVERVIEW
Use skill lessons before, during, or after reading.

Comprehension
Cause/Effect Relationships
Making Judgments

Study Skills
Alphabetical Order
Standard Book Features

Word Study
Plural Forms
Context Clues

Strategic Reading
Fix-Up Strategies

Vocabulary
boiler, p. 7
funnel, p. 7
voyage, p. 9
iceberg, p. 9
tragedy, p. 11
immigrants, p. 13
telegraph, p. 17
coward, p. 22
binoculars, p. 25
sonar, p. 30

Activity/Skill Masters
Home-School Activity Master, p. 24
Vocabulary Master, p. 25
Comprehension Skill Master: Making Judgments, p. 26
Word Study Skill Master: Context Clues, p. 27
Strategic Reading Master: Fix-Up Strategies, p. 92

For **theme-related projects**, see pages 10–11 of this Teacher's Guide.

Options for Using *Discovering the Titanic*

There are two ways in which you can use *Discovering the Titanic*. You may elect to have individuals, pairs, or small groups read independently, or you may wish to guide the instruction of each chapter more closely. Use the suggestions under **INDEPENDENT READING** with individuals, pairs, or small groups who can read the book independently. For students who need more instructional guidance, use the suggestions under **TEACHER-SUPPORTED READING**. Throughout the lesson plan, the words **independently** and **teacher support** appear in boldface type for easy identification.

Independent Reading

Before Reading
- Build Background (p. 14)
  Internet Activity
- Vocabulary Activities (p. 14)
  Vocabulary Master (p. 25)
- Book Walk (p. 15)
- Strategic Reading Master:
  Fix-Up Strategies (p. 92)

During Reading
- Setting a Purpose for Reading (p. 15)

After Reading
- Support All Learners—You may wish to have students do the challenging activity or any of the activities under Addressing Multiple Intelligences. (p. 16)
- Reader Response Activities (p. 20)
  Describing the *Titanic*
  Writing a Poem
- Curriculum Connections (p. 20)
  Learning About Ocean Liners
  Investigating Icebergs
- Skill Mini-Lessons (pp. 21–23)
  Skills Masters (pp. 26–27)

Teacher-Supported Reading

Before Reading
- Build Background (p. 14)
  Internet Activity
- Vocabulary Activities (p. 14)
  Vocabulary Master (p. 25)
- Book Walk (p. 15)
- Strategic Reading Master:
  Fix-Up Strategies (p. 92)

During Reading
- Support All Learners—Choose from among the activities for learners of varying abilities, for multiple intelligences, and for English as a second language. (p. 16)
- Setting a Purpose for Reading (p. 15)
- Chapter-by-Chapter Comprehension Checks (pp. 17–19)

After Reading
- Reader Response Activities (p. 20)
- Curriculum Connections (p. 20)
- Skill Mini-Lessons (pp. 21–23)
  Skill Masters (pp. 26–27)

Before Reading

Build Background

Write the word *Titanic* on the chalkboard and elicit from students that this is the name of a famous ship. Explain that when it set sail in 1912, it was the largest ship ever built. Discuss with students what technology existed in 1912—cars and the telegraph were new inventions. Television, satellite pictures, and computers had not yet been invented. Then ask students to share things they already know about the *Titanic*. Write students' statements in the first column of a K-W-L chart, using the headings shown below. Then have students suggest questions they may have for the second column. Students reading the book **independently** might complete the chart on their own. Work with students who need more **teacher support** to fill in the chart as you read with them.

What I Know	What I Want to Find Out	What I Learned

Internet Interested students may wish to find out more about the *Titanic* by using the following Internet addresses.

www.skarr/com/titanic

www.discovery.com/stories/science/titanic/titanic.html

members.aol.com/MNichol/Titanic.index.html.

Because of the ever-changing nature of the Internet, we suggest that you preview all referenced Internet sites before allowing students to view them.

Vocabulary Activities

Introduce the following words and definitions.

binoculars a pair of small telescopes fastened together; used with both eyes to see things far away

boiler a tank in which water is heated to make steam for power

coward a person who runs from danger or trouble

funnel a smokestack on a steamship

iceberg a huge mass of ice floating in the sea

immigrants people who move from their home country to a new home in another country

sonar an instrument that uses sound waves to find an object in deep water

telegraph an instrument used to send coded messages over wire or by radio

tragedy an event that is very sad

voyage a journey or trip taken by water

 You may wish to use the Vocabulary Master on page 25 to enhance students' understanding of the vocabulary words. These words and definitions are also listed in the Glossary on the last page of *Discovering the Titanic*.

Choose from among the following activities for additional practice with vocabulary.

Word Web
Encourage students to make a word web centering around the word *ship* and incorporating as many of the vocabulary words as possible. Suggest that they use *Discovering the Titanic* for help in completing the web.

Vocabulary Crossword
Challenge students to create a crossword, using as many of the vocabulary words as possible.

Word Hunt
Distribute newspapers or magazines. Have students work in pairs to find and circle as many of the vocabulary words as possible in an allotted time.

Book Walk

Preview and Predict Have students examine the cover and the photos in *Discovering the Titanic*. Based on the cover photo and the title, ask what they think the book will be about. Many students will have already heard of the *Titanic* because of the 1997 movie or from TV programs. Explain that *Discovering the Titanic* will give them information about how the ship sank and the efforts made to find the wreck.

Call attention to the Contents page and ask volunteers to read the chapter titles. Ask the following questions: What things would you like to know about the *Titanic*? What do you think you will learn from this book?

Strategy for Interactive Reading: Fix-Up Strategies

Explain to students that good readers adapt how fast they read to the type of material they are reading. For instance, an information-packed selection, such as *Discovering the Titanic*, requires that readers read slowly. The "fix-up strategies" of reading ahead and rereading are also helpful.

Make a copy for each student of the Strategic Reading Master on page 92 of this Teacher's Guide. Discuss with students that they may need to change how fast they read when reading some types of reading material (such as math or science). They may also want to reread sections to be sure they understand them.

For students who are reading *Discovering the Titanic* **independently**, suggest they stop after each chapter, write what they remember, and then reread the chapter at a slower rate. With students who need more **teacher support**, you may refer to the strategies of rereading as you read the book together.

Setting a Purpose for Reading

Before students begin reading *Discovering the Titanic*, ask them to read to find out new information about the *Titanic* and what life was like at the time of the *Titanic's* voyage. Encourage students who are reading **independently** to stop periodically to take notes about what they have learned.

For students who are reading with more **teacher support**, stop periodically to ask them to report on new information they've learned.

More About . . .
The *Titanic*

- The *Titanic* was 882 feet long—the length of four city blocks or nearly three football fields. It had three propellers. The middle one was 16 feet across; the other two were more than 23 feet across.

- There were 109 children on board the *Titanic*. Only 57 survived. The youngest survivors were Lilo and Lolo Navratil, French twins who were two and a half years old. They had been kidnapped by their father who went down with the ship. It took the U.S. authorities some time to locate the children's mother and return the children to her.

- Some other interesting facts are that today it would cost $400 million to build the *Titanic*, a first-class ticket on the *Titanic* cost about $4,500 in 1912 (about $50,000 today), and a third-class ticket was as low as $35.

Support All Learners

The following activities can be used during or after reading to address different learning levels and styles.

Easy
Have students measure 100 feet in the school yard or playground to get a feel for the size of the ship. Have them project how long 882 feet is–the length of the *Titanic*. Point out that the height of the ship from keel to bridge was 104 feet.

Average *(Portfolio)*
As they read chapters 4–6, have students compile a chart that shows the attempts to find the *Titanic*, including the year the attempt was made, what equipment was used, and the outcome of each attempt.

Challenging *(Portfolio)*
Encourage students to compile an "amazing facts" chart about the *Titanic*, using information from the book as well as from additional sources.

Addressing Multiple Intelligences

Visual-Spatial Learners
Help students research and find drawings or floor plans of the *Titanic*. Have them use the information to create a poster that shows the interior of the ship.

Logical-Mathematical Learners
Have students compare travel on a steamship such as the *Titanic* to travel in an airplane. Suggest they make a Venn diagram to show ways the two types of travel are different and alike.

Musical Learners *(Portfolio)*
Play the soundtrack CD from the 1997 movie *Titanic*. Invite students to paint or draw their own design for a CD cover for the album while the music is playing.

Intrapersonal Learners
Invite students to think how they might have reacted if they were passengers on the *Titanic* when it struck the iceberg. Have them write a journal entry describing their thoughts.

English as a Second Language

Students who are learning English may need help following the technical details of the searches for the ship described in the second half of the book, as well as with learning ship-related vocabulary. As often as necessary, point to details in the photographs and repeat words to help students learn terms such as *bow, stern, propeller, deck,* and *bridge*. Give special attention to words such as *stern* and *bridge* which have multiple meanings, and *bow,* which has another pronunciation. Suggest that students draw and label a simple diagram of the ship to help them remember.

During Reading

Independent Reading

For students who are reading **independently**, you may wish to make a quick check of comprehension at the midpoint and at the end of *Discovering the Titanic*, using these questions.

Midpoint

Comprehension Check
- Why was the sinking of the *Titanic* a tragedy? *(Many people lost their lives, partly because there were not enough lifeboats.)* **Critical Response**
- What is the most interesting thing you have learned about the Titanic so far? *(Answers will vary.)* **Creative Response**

End of Book

Comprehension Check
- What modern inventions helped searchers learn about the *Titanic*? *(sonar, deep-water diving subs such as* Angus *and* Argo, *video cameras)* **Critical Response**
- Do you think the wreck of the *Titanic* should be brought up from the bottom of the ocean or left alone? *(Answers will vary.)* **Creative Response**

Teacher-Supported Reading

For students who are reading with **teacher support**, use the chapter-by-chapter **Comprehension Checks** as a quick check of students' understanding. **Teachable Moments** are referenced to highlight points during reading at which you might wish to use a **Skill Mini-Lesson**. **Reader Response** questions are also provided. From time to time, you may wish to have students respond to these questions in writing.

Chapter 1 (pages 5–11)

Comprehension Check
- How can you tell that finding the *Titanic* was important to Dr. Ballard? *(He spent 12 years getting ready to search for it.)* **Critical: Making Inferences**
- On page 5 you are given the meaning of *geologist*. What is a geologist? *(a scientist who studies the earth)* **Word Study: Context Clues**

Teachable Moment *Skill Master*
This might be a good place to stop and review using context clues. The Word Study Skill Mini-Lesson on context clues is found on page 23 of this Teacher's Guide.

Reader Response
- Why do you think people are fascinated with the *Titanic*? *(Answers will vary.)* **Creative: Personal Opinion**

Chapter 2 (pages 12–18)

Comprehension Check
- Why did people think the *Titanic* was unsinkable? *(It had been designed with compartments that could be closed if they filled with water.)* **Critical: Main Idea and Details**
- Do you think the captain was in any way at fault for what happened to the *Titanic*? *(Students may agree that he should have heeded the iceberg warnings and slowed the ship.)* **Critical: Making Judgments**

Teachable Moment *Skill Master*
You may wish to use the Comprehension Skill Mini-Lesson: Making Judgments on page 21.

Reader Response
- If you were a passenger on the *Titanic*, do you think you would have felt safe? Why or why not? *(Answers will vary.)* **Creative: Personal Response**

DISCOVERING THE TITANIC

Chapter 3 (pages 19–25)

Comprehension Check
- What caused the *Titanic* to sink? *(It hit an iceberg, which ripped open the side of the ship. Then it filled with water.)* **Critical: Cause and Effect Relationships**

Teachable Moment
You may wish to review Cause and Effect Relationships with students using the Comprehension Skill Mini-Lesson on page 21.

- Why do you think people could not agree on what happened as the ship sank? *(Answers will vary, but most students will probably agree that there was confusion and not everyone saw the same thing.)* **Critical: Drawing Conclusions**

Reader Response
- Why do you think some people chose to give up their place in the lifeboats? *(Answers will vary.)* **Creative: Personal Opinion**

Chapter 4 (pages 26–32)

Comprehension Check
- What is the main idea of this chapter? *(Several attempts were made to find the Titanic, but no one was successful.)* **Critical: Main Idea**

- Why was the wreck of the *Titanic* so difficult to find? *(It went down in very deep water in a canyon which made it hard for sonar to find. The position the Titanic radioed to other ships was not exact. No one knew exactly how fast it was going when it hit the iceberg.)* **Critical: Cause and Effect Relationships**

Reader Response
- What do you think would be the most interesting part of the underwater search that Dr. Ballard did? *(Answers will vary.)* **Creative: Personal Reaction**

Chapter 5 (pages 33–37)

Comprehension Check
- What made *Argo* a better tool for searching than *Angus*? *(It had five video cameras and two sonar systems, one for the sides and one to look straight ahead.)* **Critical: Noting Details**

- An index lists topics from a book in alphabetical order. Which would come first in the index, *Argo* or *Angus*? *(Angus)* **Study Skills: Alphabetical Order**

Teachable Moment
This might be a good time to present the Study Skills Mini-Lesson on Using Alphabetical Order, on page 22 of this Teacher's Guide.

Reader Response
- How do you think you would have felt if you had been part of Dr. Ballard's team of scientists when they found the wreck of the *Titanic*? *(Answers will vary.)* **Creative: Personal Reaction**

Chapter 6 (pages 38–41)

Comprehension Check
- If you were a member of Dr. Ballard's crew when the *Titanic* was discovered, do you think you would have felt that the ship should remain undisturbed? Why or why not? **Creative: Making Judgments**

- You know that most words have a plural form to show more than one. Look at the last sentence in the first paragraph on page 40. What word is a plural form? *(mysteries)* **Word Study: Plural Forms**

Teachable Moment
You may wish to review plural forms with students at this time, using the Word Study Skill Mini-Lesson on page 23.

Reader Response
- What did you learn about the *Titanic* in this chapter that you did not know before? *(Answers will vary.)* **Creative: Personal Response**

DISCOVERING THE TITANIC—Nonfiction

Chapter 7 (pages 42–47)

Comprehension Check

- In what ways is movie director James Cameron similar to Dr. Robert Ballard? *(Both were fascinated by the* Titanic, *both had big dreams, both were very determined to achieve their goals.)* **Critical: Making Comparisons**

- If you wanted to find a description of *Argo*, what part of the book would help you find it quickly? *(the index)* **Study Skills: Standard Book Features**

Teachable Moment

You may wish to review Standard Book Features with students at this time. The Study Skills Mini-Lesson is on page 22.

Reader Response

- How might our ideas about the *Titanic* change as new discoveries about the ship and its historic voyage are made? *(Answers will vary.)* **Creative Expression**

More — English as a Second Language

Students acquiring English may benefit from extra help with organizing the information presented in the book. You may wish to create a chart or list to help students with important names introduced in the book and with information on the several expeditions to find the wreck. The chart should include the names of the searchers, dates of the expedition, outcomes of the expedition, and various inventions, such as *Alvin*, *Angus*, and *Argo*, which were used to try to locate the *Titanic*. You may wish to pair fluent with emergent English speakers to work on their charts.

After Reading

Reader Response Activities

After students have completed *Discovering the Titanic*, you may wish to choose from the following activities.

Conducting an Interview

Invite students to imagine that they could interview someone who was on the *Titanic*. Have them write questions that will help the reader know what the survivor experienced. Students may want to work in pairs to present their interviews. **Writing/Speaking**

Describing the *Titanic*

Invite students to choose their favorite photograph used in this book and write a description of what the photo shows. Challenge them to describe it well enough that someone who had not seen the photo could visualize it. **Writing**

Writing a Poem

Invite students to imagine that they have been given an opportunity to be aboard a sub such as *Argo* to visit the *Titanic* as it rests on the ocean bottom. Invite them to write a short poem that describes how they feel as they see and explore the ship. **Writing/Speaking**

CURRICULUM CONNECTIONS

Art Activity
Making a Model

Encourage interested students to create a model of the *Titanic*, using common classroom materials such as clay, construction paper, cardboard, and so on. If students prefer, they can make a diorama of one special part of the ship such as the crow's nest, the gym, the Grand Staircase, and so on. When they have finished, invite students to share their work, explaining what they have depicted and why they chose the project they did.

Science Activity
Investigating Icebergs

Have interested students research icebergs and report on their findings. Suggest they find out how and where icebergs are formed and why they are so dangerous to ships. They might also explore the technology available to ships today to prevent their running into an iceberg as the *Titanic* did.

Mathematics Activity
Discovering How Much They Paid

Allow interested students to find out the costs of first class, second class, third class, and steerage class passage on the *Titanic*, and compare the costs with travel today. Any of the Internet sites listed in this lesson will help students find information.

Social Studies Activity
Learning About Ocean Liners

Invite students to use the Internet to research other ships of the White Star Line such as the *Atlantic*, the *Britannic*, or the *Olympic*. Suggest they find out such things as the length and cost of a typical voyage, the types of foods served, the usual routes, and what happened to the ship. A related Internet site that students might be interested in is

 www.pbs.org/wgbh/nova/titanic/unsinkable.html

SKILL MINI-LESSONS

The following skill lessons may be used while or after children read the book *Discovering the Titanic*.

COMPREHENSION: Cause and Effect Relationships

Objective: To identify cause and effect relationships

Teach
Remind students that events usually have a reason, or cause, for happening. Sometimes, as with the sinking of the *Titanic*, they have more than one cause. Write the following on the chalkboard:
  The *Titanic* hit an iceberg.
  The *Titanic* sank.

Point out that the first statement is a cause, and the second statement is an effect. Explain that an effect is the result of a cause, and that a cause usually answers the question *Why?* Point out that some words such as *because* and *since* act as clues that tell there is a cause and effect relationship.

Practice
Direct students' attention to page 21. Ask them to find

- A cause that answers why many of the lifeboats left half full.
- The effect of there not being enough lifeboats for all passengers.

Evaluate
Encourage students to identify other cause and effect relationships in the remainder of the book.

COMPREHENSION: Making Judgments

Objective: To evaluate an action, character, or situation and make a decision about it based on personal knowledge and details in the text

Teach
Ask students to reread pages 17–18. Explain that when Captain Smith heard about the iceberg warnings, he may have made a judgment, or decision based on the information he had. He may have decided not to slow the ship. Point out that readers also make judgments as they read about situations or about characters' actions or motives. Good readers use information in the text and their own knowledge and experience to decide whether what the characters did was right or wrong, wise or foolish.

Practice
Have students reread page 18. Point out that the captain may not have been given the iceberg warnings or was not worried. He also probably wanted to stay on schedule because he knew arriving on time was important to the owner of the White Star Line. Ask students whether they think the captain made the right decision, and to defend their judgment based on the text and on their own knowledge.

Evaluate
You may wish to use the Comprehension Skill Master: Making Judgments on page 26 to evaluate students' understanding of this skill.

DISCOVERING THE TITANIC—Nonfiction

STUDY SKILLS: Using Alphabetical Order

Objective: To alphabetize words to the second and third letters

Teach
Recall with students that many research sources, such as encyclopedias and indexes, are arranged in alphabetical order. Write the following words on the chalkboard: *Astor*, *Alvin*, *Argo*, *Angus*. Explain that since all four words begin with *a*, to find the correct alphabetical order, students must look at the second letter. Call attention to the second letter in each word and elicit from students that the correct order is *Alvin*, *Angus*, *Argo*, *Astor*.

Repeat the procedure with the words *captain*, *crew*, *cheered*, and *control*. Elicit that *cable* would be first in an alphabetical listing.

Practice
Write the following groups of words on the chalkboard. Have students rewrite them in alphabetical order.

1. sonar   Snoop Dog   submarine
2. Titanic treasure   team
3. video   valuable   voyage

Evaluate
Have students work in pairs, writing three words that begin with the same first letter for their partner to alphabetize. Students can use a dictionary to check their work.

STUDY SKILLS: Using Standard Book Features

Objective: To locate and understand the purpose of a table of contents, an index, and a glossary

Teach
Remind students that when they previewed this book (Book Walk, p. 15), they looked at the table of contents. Have them turn to this feature again. Ask students what information the table of contents gives them. *(the numbers and titles of the chapters and the page numbers on which they begin)*

Tell students that there are two other book parts that help them find information.

- A glossary gives definitions and pronunciation of words.
- An index lists topics in alphabetical order and gives the page number in the book where that topic is found.

Explain that an index and a glossary are usually located in the back of the book.

Practice
Ask students to tell where they could look for the following information.

- the definition of *sonar* *(glossary)*
- who Margaret Brown was *(index)*
- information about *Snoop Dog* *(index)*
- the page number on which Chapter 7 begins *(table of contents)*
- the definition of *iceberg* *(glossary)*
- the title of Chapter 2 *(table of contents)*

Evaluate
Have students find and use the glossary, index, and table of contents in other books, such as a science or social studies textbook, to find specific information.

WORD STUDY: Plural Forms

Objective: To form plurals with the endings -s, -es, and -ies

Teach

Write the word *mystery* on the chalkboard and have a student read and use it in a sentence. Point out that many words have another form, a plural form that is used when meaning more than one. Write the phrase *more than one mystery* and have a volunteer write the plural form on the chalkboard. Point out that in order to make this word plural, the letter *y* is dropped and *-ies* is added. Repeat the process with the words *search, boiler,* and *discovery.* Then review the following rules:

- For most words, just add *s* to form the plural. *(boilers)*
- If a word ends in *ch, sh, x, s, x,* or *z,* add *-es. (searches)*
- If a word ends in a consonant and *y,* change the *y* to *i* and add *-es. (discoveries)*

Practice

Write the following words on the chalkboard. Call on volunteers to write the plural forms.

tragedy	sketch
discovery	lifeboat
dish	country
expert	current

Evaluate

Have students practice forming the plural form of other words that you or they locate in *Discovering the Titanic.*

WORD STUDY: Context Clues

Objective: To use context clues to determine word meaning

Teach

Write the word *geologist* on the chalkboard. Ask: If you did not know the meaning of *geologist* where could you find the meaning? Explain that students might not always have a dictionary handy and not all books have a glossary. Sometimes the word is defined in the sentence or paragraph. Call students' attention to the last sentence on page 5, to the words *scientist who studies the earth.* Point out that the word *or* and the comma are context clues that the words are a definition of *geologist.*

Next, have students turn to page 14 and reread the paragraph. Explain that the definition of *watertight* is not given directly, but readers can figure it out from the context.

Practice

Write the following on the chalkboard.

- Until 1973, the *Alvin* could not dive very deep because its <u>hull</u>, or frame, was not strong enough.
- The *Argo* located the <u>bow</u>, or front part of the ship.

Have students use the context to tell what the underlined words mean. Then ask them to explain what part of the sentence helped them figure out the meanings.

Evaluate

You may wish to use Study Skills Master: Context Clues to evaluate students' understanding of this skill.

Home-School Connection

Dear Family,

Our class is reading chapter books about discoveries. The book we are currently reading is *Discovering the Titanic* by Cindy Trumbore. It tells the story of the sinking of the *Titanic* and the efforts made to find the wreck.

Discover Together

- You may want to go to the local library to help your child find out more about the *Titanic* or other sunken ships. Here are some books to look for:

    Sunken Treasure by Gail Gibbons, (Harper Collins, 1990)

    Ships by Donna Bailey (Steck-Vaughn, 1990)

- Watch together any of the many movies made about the sinking of the *Titanic*, such as *Titanic* (1997) and *A Night to Remember* (1958).

Conexión con el hogar

Estimada familia:

En este capítulo, nuestra clase esta leyendo libros que están relacionados con descubrimientos. El libro que estamos leyendo en la actualidad se titula *Discovering the Titanic* de Cindy Trumbore, que narra la historia del hundimiento del *Titanic* y los esfuerzos para hallar los restos del naufragio.

Descubran juntos

- Pueden visitar la biblioteca local para ayudar a su hijo/a a conocer más acerca del *Titanic* u otros naufragios marítimos. Estos son algunos de los libros que pueden buscar:

    Sunken Treasure de Gail Gibbons (HarperCollins, 1990)

    Ships de Donna Bailey (Steck-Vaughn, 1990)

- Vean juntos cualquiera de las varias películas hechas sobre el hundimiento del *Titanic* tales como *Titanic* (1997) y *A Night to Remember* (1958).

VOCABULARY MASTER

Name _____

 Vocabulary: Glossary Words

Choose a vocabulary word from the box that correctly completes each sentence and write it on the line.

| binoculars | funnel | boiler | coward | iceberg |
| tragedy | sonar | telegraph | immigrants | voyage |

1. The _____ heated the water to make steam.

2. Smoke poured out of each _____ on the ship.

3. The *Titanic* was getting ready for its first _____.

4. Many of the third-class passengers were _____, hoping to start a new life in America.

5. Some people watched through _____ as the ship left port.

6. Meantime, a huge _____ was drifting in the cold Atlantic.

7. No one realized the voyage would end in _____.

8. One person would act bravely, while another would be a _____.

9. News of the disaster would travel around the world by a recent invention, the _____.

10. The wreck of the *Titanic* would not be found until the invention of _____.

DISCOVERING THE TITANIC—Nonfiction

SKILL MASTER

Name _____

Comprehension: Making Judgments

Readers often make decisions or judgments about what they read, based on what the text tells them and what they know from their own knowledge or experience.

Reread page 43 of *Discovering the Titanic*. Then read the judgments below and select the one that seems most sensible.

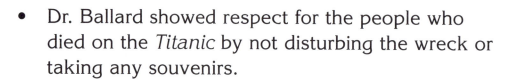

- Dr. Ballard showed respect for the people who died on the *Titanic* by not disturbing the wreck or taking any souvenirs.

- Dr. Ballard did not care anything about the people who died on the *Titanic*. He only wanted to be famous for discovering it.

Explain the choice you made. Use evidence from the book and your own knowledge and experience.

_____
_____
_____
_____
_____
_____
_____

SKILL MASTER

Name _____

Word Study: Context Clues

You can figure out the meaning of many new words by using context clues. This means that the words in the sentences around the unfamiliar word help you understand its meaning.

Read the sentences. Then fill in the circle next to the best meaning for the underlined word.

1. Dr. Ballard decided to look for the <u>debris</u> field, or trail of objects that would have fallen from the sinking ship.

    ○ a kind of sonar   ○ litter; things   ○ footprints

2. Jack Grimm had looked for other <u>fabled</u> things such as Noah's Ark and the Loch Ness Monster. Their stories interested him.

    ○ sunken   ○ told about in stories   ○ monsters

3. The <u>pressure</u> of deep water could crush the hull of the sub.

    ○ hardness   ○ force   ○ saltiness

Write a meaning for the underlined word, using context clues.

   There was a lot of <u>confusion</u> as people were told to board the lifeboats. Everyone was running around, lifeboats were leaving when they were only half full, and no one knew where to go.

_____

_____

_____

DISCOVERING THE TITANIC—Nonfiction

THROUGH THE GARDEN DOOR

DISCOVERIES: BOOK 17

GENRE: FANTASY

Summary

It is winter in the city and Jason and his friend Miko are walking home from school, wishing they could travel to some place warm. Suddenly, they spot an unusual animal moving cautiously along the sidewalk. They follow it through a doorway and find themselves in a beautiful garden. Nothing is as it seems in this unusual place. The garden's caretaker tells them they can return if they tell no one about the existence of the garden. Miko and Jason do their best to keep the Gardener's secret, but when they leave the garden with one of its seeds, they realize that even though they love the garden, a sacrifice must be made so the garden can live on.

Home-School Connection

The Home-School activity master on page 40 of this Teacher's Guide provides a variety of activities students can do at home with family members.

PLANNER

SKILLS OVERVIEW
Use skill lessons before, during, or after reading.

Comprehension
Imagery
Author's Craft
Making Predictions
Setting

Study Skills
Following Directions

Word Study
Suffixes

Strategic Reading
Visualizing

Vocabulary
curious, p. 9
exotic, p. 10
ordinary, p. 16
protect, p. 23
promise, p. 24
personality, p. 26
shock, p. 38
mistake, p. 39
grate, p. 47
suspicious, p. 51

Activity/Skill Masters
Home-School Activity Master, p. 40
Vocabulary Master, p. 41
Comprehension Skill Master: Imagery, p. 42
Comprehension Skill Master: Making Predictions, p. 43
Strategic Reading Master: Visualizing, p. 93

For **theme-related projects**, see pages 10–11 of this Teacher's Guide.

Options for Using *Through the Garden Door*

There are two ways in which you can use *Through the Garden Door*. You may elect to have individuals, pairs, or small groups read independently, or you may wish to guide the instruction of each chapter more closely. Use the suggestions under **INDEPENDENT READING** with individuals, pairs, or small groups who can read the book independently. For students who need more instructional guidance, use the suggestions under **TEACHER-SUPPORTED READING**. Throughout the lesson plan, the words **independently** and **teacher support** appear in boldface type for easy identification.

Independent Reading	Teacher-Supported Reading
Before Reading • Build Background (p. 30) 　Internet Activity • Vocabulary Activities (p. 30) 　Vocabulary Master (p. 41) • Book Walk (p. 31) • Strategic Reading Master: 　Visualizing (p. 93)	**Before Reading** • Build Background (p. 30) 　Internet Activity • Vocabulary Activities (p. 30) 　Vocabulary Master (p. 41) • Book Walk (p. 31) • Strategic Reading Master: 　Visualizing (p. 93)
During Reading • Setting a Purpose for Reading (p. 31)	**During Reading** • Support All Learners—Choose from among the activities for learners of varying abilities, for multiple intelligences, and for English as a second language. (p. 32) • Setting a Purpose for Reading (p. 31) • Chapter-by-Chapter Comprehension Checks (pp. 33–35)
After Reading • Support All Learners—You may wish to have students do the challenging activity or any of the activities under Addressing Multiple Intelligences. (p. 32) • Reader Response Activities (p. 36) 　Describing a Plant or Animal 　Making a Nature Fact Sheet • Curriculum Connections (p. 36) 　Writing a Newspaper Story 　Gardens Around the World 　Plotting and Fencing the Garden • Skill Mini-Lessons (pp. 37–39) 　Skill Masters (pp. 42–43)	**After Reading** • Reader Response Activities (p. 36) • Curriculum Connections (p. 36) • Skill Mini-Lessons (pp. 37–39) 　Skill Masters (pp. 42–43)

THROUGH THE GARDEN DOOR—Fantasy

Before Reading

Build Background

Ask students if they have ever visited an arboretum or some other kind of public or botanical garden. Encourage students to describe the kinds of plants and trees they saw there. Did they spot any kinds of plants that they had never seen before? What did they look like? What made them different from plants they might see in someone's backyard garden? Invite students to help you organize the information on a chart, using the headings shown below. Students reading the book **independently** might create their own chart and add to it as they read. Allow students who need more **teacher support** while reading to suggest facts to add to the chart as you read with them.

VISIT TO A GARDEN		
Kinds of Plants	Color	Shape
1.	1.	1.
2.	2.	2.

Internet Interested students may wish to find out more about botanical gardens and arboretums by using the following Internet addresses.

commtechlab.msu.edu/
sites/garden/overview.html

www.seerockcity.com/
photgall.html

Because of the ever-changing nature of the Internet, we suggest that you preview all referenced Internet sites before allowing students to view them.

Vocabulary Activities

Introduce the following words and definitions.

curious wanting very much to know something

exotic strange and different

grate a metal frame with bars set in the street to cover a water drain

mistake an act that is wrong; an error

ordinary usual, common; not special in any way

personality the special qualities that make a person different from another person

promise an agreement to do or not to do something

protect to guard or defend against harm or danger

shock to upset the mind or feelings with sudden force

suspicious feeling or showing the belief that something is wrong

 You may wish to use the Vocabulary Master on page 41 to enhance students' understanding of the vocabulary words. These words and definitions are also listed in the Glossary on the last page of *Through the Garden Door*.

Choose from among the following activities for additional practice with vocabulary.

Crossword Puzzle Have students make up a crossword puzzle using as many of the vocabulary words as possible.

Vocabulary Story Ask students to use as many of the vocabulary words as possible in an original story.

Journal Entry Ask students to use as many of the vocabulary words as possible in a journal entry in which they write as if they were one of the characters in the story.

Book Walk

Preview and Predict Explain to students that *Through the Garden Door* is a fantasy. It is set in the present and portrays realistic characters who share an experience that could not happen in real life.

Invite students to describe what they see on the cover of *Through the Garden Door*. Then encourage them to read the chapter titles on the Contents page. Ask the following question: What do chapter titles such as The Chase Begins, The Garden, The Big Mistake, and Saving the Garden reveal about what happens in this story?

Strategy for Interactive Reading: Visualizing

Visualizing the plot is a good strategy for students to use as they read *Through the Garden Door*. Make a copy for each student of the Strategic Reading Master on page 93 of this Teacher's Guide. Explain that the plot is the series of actions or events that happen in a story, including the main problem, what leads up to solving the problem, and the solution. Model how to recognize a plot problem in Chapter 1 of *Through the Garden Door*.

Walking home from school one day, Miko and Jason spot a strange animal. They try to get close, but the animal manages to stay ahead. Finally, it slips inside an open door. How will Miko and Jason solve their problem?

If students are reading *Through the Garden Door* **independently**, have them identify a problem the characters face, and its possible solution, after reading each chapter. Help students who need more **teacher support** to use the chapter title as a focus and guide them to look for clues to help them recognize the story problem.

Setting a Purpose for Reading

Ask students to read the first two pages of *Through the Garden Door*. Then ask them where they think Miko and Jason might live, and whether they will be able to escape the cold weather. Encourage students who are reading **independently** to stop periodically to set their own purpose for reading on.

For students who are reading with more **teacher support**, vary the ways in which you set a purpose for reading. For example, you may wish to ask students to read further to find out information based on chapter titles or to preview the illustrations and make informed guesses about what the characters are doing, and what happens to them. They can then read to see if they were correct.

More About . . .
Gardens

The Hanging Gardens of Babylon were probably built by King Nebuchadnezzar II and were one of the Seven Wonders of the Ancient World. Babylon was located near the modern city of Baghdad, in Iraq, and Nebuchadnezzar ruled from 605 to 562 B.C. Our information about the gardens comes from an account by Berossus, a Babylonian priest. He described gardens laid out on a brick terrace about 400 feet square and 75 feet above the ground.

THROUGH THE GARDEN DOOR—Fantasy

Support All Learners

The following activities can be used during or after reading to address different learning levels and styles.

Easy

Remind students that as Miko and Jason explore the garden, they find flowers that smell like cookies and strawberries. Invite students to find these descriptions in the text. Then encourage them to draw pictures of other types of flowers that the children might have found as they continued to explore the garden.

Average

Remind students that Jason fantasizes about escaping the cold weather by heading to a faraway planet where it never snows. Invite students to write a description of the planet Jason would like to travel to, the kinds of plants and animals that might be found there, and what the weather would be like.

Challenging

Invite students to write a continuation of the story in which they explain more about what happens to Miko and Jason and the garden.

Addressing Multiple Intelligences

Verbal-Linguistic Learners

Invite students to write short poems celebrating a favorite kind of garden plant. It might be a flower or a tree. Students may wish to find or draw a picture of the plant and attach it to the poem. Collect the poems in a book for classmates to share.

Logical-Mathematical Learners

Students who enjoy working with numbers might enjoy making a schedule for one of Miko and Jason's visits to the garden. Ask students to name some of the activities Miko and Jason engage in as they help the Gardener. Before students make their final schedule, have them discuss how long each activity would take.

Bodily-Kinesthetic Learners

Encourage students to make a diorama of the garden. They can use clay or make small cardboard replicas of the characters, plants, trees, and objects.

English as a Second Language

Verbs such as *blurted*, *stammered*, *chattered*, and *gasped* may present a problem for students whose first language is not English. Have students look for details in the illustrations that can help them understand words in the text. Clarify for students that these words are all verbs that can be used in place of the word *said*. Pantomime words such as *gasped* and *scolded* and then have students pantomime them. Explain that these words can be used in place of *said* to reveal the emotions of the characters in the story.

THROUGH THE GARDEN DOOR—Fantasy

During Reading

Independent Reading
For students who are reading **independently**, you may wish to make a quick check of comprehension at the midpoint and at the end of *Through the Garden Door*, using these questions.

Midpoint
Comprehension Check
- Do you think Miko and Jason will be able to keep the garden a secret? *(Answers may vary but should include that the children want to visit the garden again, so they will try to keep it a secret.)* **Critical Response**
- Who do you think created the garden? *(Answers will vary.)* **Creative Response**

End of Book
Comprehension Check
- Why do you think the entire garden would die if only one plant from the garden began to grow in the outside world? *(Answers will vary.)* **Critical Response**
- Do you think Miko and Jason will visit the garden again one day? Why or why not? *(Answers will vary.)* **Creative Response**

Teacher-Supported Reading
For students who are reading with **teacher support**, use the chapter-by-chapter Comprehension Checks as a quick check of students' understanding. Teachable Moments are referenced to highlight points during reading at which you might wish to use a Skill Mini-Lesson. Reader Response questions are also provided. From time to time, you may wish to have students respond to these questions in writing.

Chapter 1 (pages 5–12)
Comprehension Check
- What do Jason and Miko's ideas for escaping the cold weather tell you about their characters? *(Jason has a great imagination. Miko is more practical.)* **Critical: Making Comparisons**
- What do you think is on the other side of the door? *(Students should predict that it is a garden.)* **Critical: Making Predictions**

Teachable Moment *Skill Master*
You may wish to use the Comprehension Skill Mini-Lesson: Making Predictions. It is located on page 38.

Reader Response
- Would you have followed the strange animal? Why or why not? *(Answers will vary.)* **Creative: Personal Response**

Chapter 2 (pages 13–17)
Comprehension Check
- Who do you think the woman who speaks to Miko and Jason might be? *(She must be someone who takes care of the garden.)* **Critical: Making Inferences**
- What descriptive words help you know that the garden is pleasant? *(The air felt soft and warm; a light breeze tickled their noses; bright flowers grew everywhere.)* **Critical: Imagery**

Teachable Moment *Skill Master*
You may wish to use the Comprehension Skill Mini-Lesson: Imagery. It is located on page 37.

Reader Response
- How would you feel if you discovered the garden? *(Answers will vary.)* **Creative: Personal Response**

Chapter 3 (pages 18–25)

Comprehension Check
- What do you think Miko and Jason will find as they explore the garden? *(They will probably find more strange plants and animals that they would not find in the outside world.)* **Critical: Predicting Outcomes**
- Onomatopoeia is the use of words that imitate sounds. Where can you find onomatopoeia in this chapter? *(The words that describe the sound of the chatter-chee: "Chitt. Chitt. Chee.")* **Critical: Author's Craft**

Teachable Moment
You may find this a good time to use the Comprehension Skill Mini-Lesson: Author's Craft. You will find it on page 37.

Reader Response
- What other name might you think of for the animal the Gardener calls a chatter-chee? *(Answers will vary.)* **Creative: Creative Expression**

Chapter 4 (pages 26–30)

Comprehension Check
- In what way is the garden different from gardens you would find in the real world? *(The plants, trees, and animals seem to have personalities of their own; the animals look different.)* **Critical: Drawing Conclusions**
- What directions must Miko and Jason remember if they want to return to the garden? *(They must knock on the door three times, wait exactly one minute, and then knock three more times.)* **Study Skills: Following Directions**

Teachable Moment
To clarify the process of following oral directions, you may want to use the Study Skills Mini-Lesson: Following Directions, on page 39.

Reader Response
- Do you think you would want to work as the garden's caretaker? Why or why not? *(Answers will vary.)* **Creative: Personal Opinion**

Chapter 5 (pages 31–38)

Comprehension Check
- What do you think the Gardener means when she says that it's "garden time"? *(Answers may vary but will probably include that it's time for the Gardener to go to work or that time is different in the garden than outside.)* **Critical: Drawing Conclusions**
- What are two places described in the story? *(the city where Miko and Jason live and the garden)* **Critical: Setting**

Teachable Moment
You may find this a good time to use the Comprehension Skill Mini-Lesson: Setting. You will find it on page 38.

Reader Response
- What names would you give the flowers that Miko and Jason have seen in the garden? *(Answers will vary.)* **Creative: Personal Expression**

Chapter 6 (pages 39–45)

Comprehension Check
- Why do you think the Gardener warned Miko and Jason not to take anything from the garden? *(Everything in the garden is special. It might be dangerous if unusual seeds were planted in the outside world.)* **Critical: Making Inferences**
- Why does Miko put the box with the seeds under her pillow? *(Answers may vary but should include that she was keeping the seeds safe and making sure that no one would see them.)* **Critical: Cause and Effect**
- What do you think happened to the missing seed? *(Answers may include that the wind may have blown one of the seeds out of the box.)* **Critical: Drawing Conclusions**

Reader Response
- If you were Miko, would you have told the Gardener what happened with the seeds? Why or why not? *(Answers will vary.)*

THROUGH THE GARDEN DOOR—Fantasy

Chapter 7 (pages 46–55)

Comprehension Check
- In what ways is Kim a danger to the garden? *(She has seen a plant from the garden. She also saw Jason and Miko go through the garden door.)* **Critical: Making Inferences**
- The suffix *-er* means "a person who does or makes something." How does the suffix help you figure out the meaning of the word *Gardener* on page 54? To what word has the suffix been added? *(Garden. The suffix helps you know that the gardener is "one who gardens.")* **Word Study: Suffixes**

Teachable Moment
You may wish to use the Word Study Skill Mini-Lesson: Suffixes. You will find it on page 39.

Reader Response
- What would you tell Kim if she asked you about the mysterious plant? *(Answers will vary.)* **Creative: Personal Reaction**

Chapter 8 (pages 56–63)

Comprehension Check
- How do you think the Gardener might get back in touch with Miko and Jason? *(Answers will vary.)* **Critical: Predicting Outcomes**
- Why do you think the garden door disappeared one day and new bricks blocked the space where the door had been? *(Answers may vary but will probably include that the garden will be protected.)* **Critical: Drawing Conclusions**
- Do you think that Miko's and Jason's decision not to return to the garden was a good one? Why or why not? *(Answers will vary.)* **Critical: Making Judgments**

Reader Response
- Do you think Miko and Jason will ever visit the garden again? Why or why not? *(Answers will vary.)* **Creative: Personal Opinion**

More: English as a Second Language

Students acquiring English may benefit from a review of synonyms and antonyms. Explain that synonyms are words that mean the same thing or almost the same thing, such as *smell* and *odor*. Antonyms are words that have opposite meanings, such as *remember* and *forget*.

Students of varying language proficiency can work in pairs to find synonyms and antonyms in the story.

THROUGH THE GARDEN DOOR—Fantasy

After Reading

Reader Response Activities

After students have completed *Through the Garden Door,* you may wish to choose from the following activities.

Writing a Daily Planner

Invite students to work with a partner to write the Gardener's daily planner. The planner can take the form of a daily list of activities and responsibilities. Suggest that student pairs exchange planners with other pairs after they finish to compare activities. **Writing**

Describing a Plant or Animal

Invite students to write their own descriptions of at least one garden animal or plant on an index card. Then divide the class into two teams. Let each team pull a card from the deck and complete the sentence "I'm thinking of something that . . ." **Writing/Listening/Speaking**

Making a Nature Fact Sheet

Have students brainstorm a list of things they enjoy about nature. Then have them identify one thing they would most like to preserve. Ask them to write a title on a sheet of paper and include facts about what it is, how it is enjoyed, and why it should be preserved. **Writing**

CURRICULUM CONNECTIONS

Drama Activity
Creating a Skit

Provide materials for students to make animal masks or costumes such as paper bags, paper plates, construction paper, oaktag, string, scissors, and markers. Have students work in groups to create skits about what would happen if all the garden animals escaped into the snowy city streets. How would people react? Allow students time to make their masks and costumes and to present their skits.

Language Arts Activity
Writing a Newspaper Story

Ask students to imagine that Kim uncovered the secret of the garden and now newspaper reporters are coming from all over to write about the discovery. Remind students to answer the questions Who? What? When? Where? and Why? as they write their news stories. Encourage them to come up with their own ideas about who created the garden, how old it is, and the identity of the Gardener.

Geography Activity
Gardens Around the World

Invite interested students to find out more about different famous parks and gardens, such as those at Versailles, or Central Park in New York. Students can use an encyclopedia or other reference sources to create a chart or list of these gardens with facts such as their size, when they were created, and who designed them. A related Internet site is

www.giverny.org/gardens/fcm/visitgb.htm

Mathematics Activity
Plotting and Fencing a Garden

Ask students to draw a possible shape for the garden, using straight lines. Students can use rulers to draw the shape, adding features such as grassy areas and trees. Explain that the garden's perimeter is the measurement of its boundary. Ask students to find the perimeter and to explain how they measured it.

THROUGH THE GARDEN DOOR—Fantasy

Skill Mini-Lessons

The following skill lessons may be used while or after students read the book *Through the Garden Door*.

COMPREHENSION: Imagery

Objective: To recognize words that appeal to the senses

Teach
Have students turn to page 15 in *Through the Garden Door* and reread the first paragraph on the page. Then explain to students that authors often use words that appeal to the senses. These words help the reader to see, hear, touch, taste, or smell what an author is describing. Point out the sentences *The air felt soft and warm* and *A light breeze tickled their noses* from the paragraph on page 15. Then ask students what sense these words appeal to. Have them pick out other sensory words in the paragraph.

Practice
As students read, ask them to find other examples of sensory language in the story. Have them use the examples to fill in the chart below.

SENSORY WORD	SENSE IT APPEALS TO	WHAT IT DESCRIBES
1.	1.	1.
2.	2.	2.
3.	3.	3.

Evaluate
You may wish to use the Comprehension Skill Master: Imagery to evaluate students' understanding of the skill.

COMPREHENSION: Author's Craft

Objective: To identify the use of figurative language in a story

Teach
Explain to students that figurative language appeals to a reader's imagination and feelings and helps the reader to visualize what is happening in the story. Point out that there are many types of figurative language. A simile is a comparison of two unlike things, using the words *like* or *as*. In *Through the Garden Door*, the author says that the ground was "springy like a thick carpet." This helps the reader to visualize the grass.

When an author uses personification, something not human is given human attributes: for example, the "cold air greeted them in a rush."

Onomatopoeia is the use of words that imitate sounds, like the call that the chatter-chee makes.

Practice
Have students identify the following phrases as examples of personification, onomatopoeia, or simile.
The grass was as green as emeralds.
Vroom! We heard the loud sound of a motor-cycle.
The sun peeked out from behind the clouds.

Evaluate
Have students work with a partner to identify at least one example of personification, onomatopoeia, and simile in the story.

COMPREHENSION: Making Predictions

Objective: To identify clues in the text to figure out what might happen next

Teach

Explain that using picture clues, text clues, and prior knowledge to guess what will happen in a story is called making predictions. Explain that predictions can be confirmed or changed by reading further in the story. Have students look through the chapter titles of *Through the Garden Door*. Point out that the chapter title "The Big Mistake," for example, is a text clue that could help them predict that Miko and Jason might break one of the Gardener's rules.

Practice

Have students reread the last page in Chapter 1 of the book. Ask them to predict what they think will happen next. Will Jason and Miko follow the animal through the door? If they do, what will they find on the other side? Provide students with the choices below and ask them to select one as a prediction of what might happen. Students should support their prediction with clues from the text. Have them read on to check their predictions.

- Miko and Jason open the door and find a garden.
- Miko and Jason open the door and find a warehouse.

Evaluate

You may wish to use Comprehension Skill Master: Making Predictions to evaluate students' understanding of the skill.

COMPREHENSION: Setting

Objective: To understand the importance of the setting in a story

Teach

Explain to students that the setting of a story is the location and time in which it takes place. The place can be real or make-believe. The time can be the past, present, or future. Point out that clues such as clothing, weather, animals, and buildings can help students determine the setting of a story. Invite students to talk about the various settings in *Through the Garden Door* and tell how they affect Miko and Jason. Clarify that knowing the setting of a story can help readers to picture the story in their minds and also help explain how the characters in the story feel.

Practice

Create two word webs for the settings in the story, one labeled "The Garden" and the other labeled "Outside the Garden." Have students complete the word webs, comparing and contrasting what they know about the two settings in the story.

Evaluate

After students finish reading the book, encourage them to compare and contrast the setting of the garden with the setting of the park in the springtime at the end of the story. Suggest that they make a chart showing the similarities and differences between the two settings.

STUDY SKILLS: Following Directions

Objective: To understand the importance of following directions

Teach
Discuss with students whether they have ever had to follow a set of directions in order to make something, such as a sandwich or a model figure. Call on volunteers to discuss what would happen if they left out a step. Then ask students why it is important to follow directions. Point out that directions can be oral or written and must be followed completely to know how to do or make something or how to get somewhere. Then ask what kind of directions Miko and Jason had to follow in order to get into the garden.

Practice
Give the following sets of oral directions to students. Then have them follow the directions in order as a group.

1. Stand up. Turn around. Sit down.
2. Put your hands on your head. Touch your knees. Stamp your foot one time.
3. Hop on your right foot. Jump on both feet. Hop on your left foot.

Evaluate
Have students write a new set of directions for gaining admission to the garden. Have students share their directions when they have finished.

WORD STUDY: Suffixes

Objective: To identify words with suffixes

Teach
Remind students of the meaning of the suffix *-er* in the word *Gardener* on page 54. (*one who gardens*) Explain to students that a suffix is added to the end of a base word. Point out that the suffixes *-y, -ly,* and *-er* are common suffixes to look for. Have students turn to the top of page 5 of *Through the Garden Door* and read the first paragraph on the page. Ask what suffix has been added to the word *ice* in the paragraph. (*-y*) Point out that the suffix *-y* means "full of, or covered with." Call on volunteers to explain how this suffix helps them to understand the meaning of the word *icy*. ("full of, or covered with, ice"). Then have them look at the last paragraph on page 47. Ask what suffix has been added to the word *faint*. (*-ly*) Explain that the suffix *-ly* means "of, or like;" "in a certain way." Have a volunteer explain the meaning of *faintly*. (*in a faint way*)

Practice
Have students practice separating base words from suffixes with the following words from the book.

    fuzzy   gently   gardener

Have them explain how the suffix changes the meaning of the base word.

Evaluate
Have students work in pairs to conduct a *-y, -ly,* and *-er,* suffix search. One student has five minutes to search the book for suffixes. Then the other student must take the list and divide the words into base words and suffixes.

THROUGH THE GARDEN DOOR—Fantasy

Home-School Connection

Dear Family,

Our class is reading chapter books that have to do with discoveries. The book we are currently reading is *Through the Garden Door* by Barbara Reeves. It tells about two children, Miko and Jason, who discover an unusual garden in the middle of a cold, dreary winter.

Discover Together

- You may want to go to the local library to help your child find more books about gardens. Here are some books to look for.

    The Secret Garden by Frances Hodgson Burnett (HarperCollins, 1987)

    Garden by Robert Maass (Holt, 1998)

- Check your local video store for movies about strange and fantastic places, such as *The Wizard of Oz*.

Conexión con el hogar

Estimada familia:

En este capítulo, nuestra clase está leyendo libros que están relacionados con descubrimientos. El libro que estamos leyendo en la actualidad se titula *Through the Garden Door* de Barbara Reeves, que trata sobre dos niños, Miko y Jason, que descubren un jardín de sorpresas en medio de un frío y triste invierno.

Descubran juntos

- Pueden visitar la biblioteca local para ayudar a su hijo/a a conocer más acerca de jardines. Estos son algunos de los libros que pueden buscar:

    The Secret Garden de Frances Hodgson Burnett (HarperCollins, 1987)

    Garden de Robert Maass (Holt, 1998)

- Busquen en la tienda de vídeos local películas sobre lugares extradinarios y fantásticos tales como *The Wizard of Oz*.

THROUGH THE GARDEN DOOR—Fantasy

Name _____

 Vocabulary: Glossary Words

Use the words from the box to finish the sentences below.

| curious | exotic | grate | mistake | ordinary |
| personality | promise | protect | shock | suspicious |

1. "It was a _____ to leave before the snow stopped," said Carlos. "My hair got all wet."

2. Cindy was very _____ about the plants in the garden and asked the gardener many questions.

3. After watching a movie in a cool theater, walking out on the hot city streets can be quite a _____.

4. We saw many strange and _____ flowers.

5. Willy always wears gloves during the winter to _____ his hands from the cold.

6. People like Belle because of her great _____.

7. Lon accidentally dropped a quarter into a _____ in the sidewalk.

8. Daria gave Joey a _____ look when he hid the flower behind his back.

9. Celia said she wouldn't tell anyone, and you can count on her to keep her _____.

10. When Pete saw the huge flowers in the yard, he knew that this was not an _____ garden.

SKILL MASTER

Name _____

Comprehension: Imagery

Imagery is descriptive language that appeals to one of the five senses.

Each sentence below contains imagery. Read the sentence and write whether the imagery appeals to the sense of sight, sound, taste, smell, or touch.

_____ 1. The sad sound of the foghorn pierced the quiet city street.

_____ 2. The chatter-chee's eyes glowed like hot coals in the dark.

_____ 3. The flowers in the garden filled the air with the scent of cookies.

_____ 4. The cold air greeted them with a slap in the face.

_____ 5. An explosion filled the ballpark as the batter hit a home run.

_____ 6. The soft breeze tickled his nose and made him sneeze.

_____ 7. The apples looked like shining rubies in the afternoon sun.

_____ 8. The cold water was as sweet as honey after their long walk in the desert.

_____ 9. The lake was a shiny piece of glass in the deep forest.

_____ 10. Margaret's voice was as soft as velvet as she spoke to the frightened dog.

©MCP All rights reserved. Copying of this page is permitted.

42　THROUGH THE GARDEN DOOR—Fantasy

SKILL MASTER

Name _____

Comprehension: Making Predictions

To make a prediction, use story clues and what you already know to guess what will happen next in a story.

Read the predictions for *Through the Garden Door*. Then read the questions about the predictions. Fill in the circles next to your answers.

Prediction 1

Miko and Jason will follow the strange animal through the doorway.

Which clue from the story helps you make this prediction?

- ○ a. Miko and Jason are very curious to find out what the animal is.
- ○ b. Miko and Jason want to get out of the cold.
- ○ c. Miko and Jason want to keep the animal as a pet.

What do you already know that helps you make this prediction?

- ○ a. Everybody hates winter weather.
- ○ b. Most people are curious.
- ○ c. Most people like pets.

Prediction 2

Miko and Jason will return to the garden a second time.

Which clue from the story helps you make this prediction?

- ○ a. Jason says he can't wait until tomorrow.
- ○ b. Miko and Jason are on vacation from school.
- ○ c. Miko wants to pick flowers.

What do you already know that helps you make this prediction?

- ○ a. Most people would like a warm place in the winter.
- ○ b. Most people like flowers.
- ○ c. People on vacation like to find something to do.

THROUGH THE GARDEN DOOR—Fantasy

DISCOVERIES: BOOK 18
ON THE WAY TO THE MOON
GENRE: NONFICTION

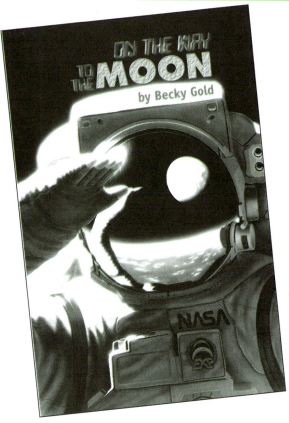

Summary

On the Way to the Moon gives students a look at the moon from a variety of perspectives—historical, mythical, and scientific. Included are some of the stories ancient people told to explain why the moon is in the sky and information about how early scientists began to learn more with the help of telescopes. In the last half century, human beings have landed on the moon, and the rocks they brought back tell us much more about our nearest celestial neighbor. Spacecraft have surveyed the moon for even more information about its history and the possibility of using the moon as a base for humankind's exploration of outer space.

Home-School Connection

The Home-School activity master on page 56 of this Teacher's Guide provides a variety of activities students can do at home with family members.

PLANNER

SKILLS OVERVIEW
Use skill lessons before, during, or after reading.

Comprehension
Classify/Categorize
Paraphrasing

Study Skills
Graphic Aids—Diagram
Locating Sources of Information

Word Study
Analogies
Inflected Forms

Strategic Reading
Self-Assess

Vocabulary
Fahrenheit, p. 12
orbit, p. 13
axis, p. 13
astronaut, p. 14
phase, p. 18
eclipse, p. 20
crater, p. 32
meteor, p. 32
comet, p. 32
solar system, p. 44

Activity/Skill Masters
Home-School Activity Master, p. 56
Vocabulary Master, p. 57
Comprehension Skill Master: Classify/Categorize, p. 58
Word Study Master: Analogies, p. 59
Strategic Reading Master: Self-Assess, p. 94

For **theme-related projects**, see pages 10–11 of this Teacher's Guide.

Options for Using *On the Way to the Moon*

There are two ways in which you can use *On the Way to the Moon*. You may elect to have individuals, pairs, or small groups read independently, or you may wish to guide the instruction of each chapter more closely. Use the suggestions under **INDEPENDENT READING** with individuals, pairs, or small groups who can read the book independently. For students who need more instructional guidance, use the suggestions under **TEACHER-SUPPORTED READING**. Throughout the lesson plan, the words **independently** and **teacher support** appear in boldface type for easy identification.

Independent Reading

Before Reading
- Build Background (p. 46)
  Internet Activity
- Vocabulary Activities (p. 46)
  Vocabulary Master (p. 57)
- Book Walk (p. 47)
- Strategic Reading Master:
  Self-Assess (p. 94)

During Reading
- Setting a Purpose for Reading (p. 47)

After Reading
- Support All Learners—You may wish to have students do the challenging activity or any of the activities under Addressing Multiple Intelligences. (p. 48)
- Reader Response Activities (p. 52)
  Writing a Journal Entry
  Drawing a Mythical Character
- Curriculum Connections (p. 52)
  Making Spacecraft Models
  Creating a Myth
  Making a Time Line
- Skill Mini-Lessons (pp. 53–55)
  Skill Masters (pp. 58–59)

Teacher-Supported Reading

Before Reading
- Build Background (p. 46)
  Internet Activity
- Vocabulary Activities (p. 46)
  Vocabulary Master (p. 57)
- Book Walk (p. 47)
- Strategic Reading Master:
  Self-Assess (p. 94)

During Reading
- Support All Learners—Choose from among the activities for learners of varying abilities, for multiple intelligences, and for English as a second language. (p. 48)
- Setting a Purpose for Reading (p. 47)
- Chapter-by-Chapter Comprehension Checks (pp. 49–51)

After Reading
- Reader Response Activities (p. 52)
- Curriculum Connections (p. 52)
- Skill Mini-Lessons (pp. 53–55)
  Skill Masters (pp. 58–59)

Before Reading

Build Background

Discuss with students what they know about the moon from books, movies, or their own observations. Ask them to think about the following: What were some of the things early people believed about the moon? Which of these ideas are really true? Have students organize a Belief/Truth chart about the moon like the one below. Students reading the book independently might create their own chart and add to it as they read. Allow students who need more **teacher support** to suggest Belief/Truth entries to add to the chart as you read with them.

Belief	Truth
The moon has a woman, a toad, or a man on it.	The moon has light and dark areas that have interesting shapes.
The moon causes tides on the earth.	The moon causes tides on the earth.

Internet Interested students may wish to find out more about the moon by using the following Internet addresses.

www.windows.umich.edu/the_universe/uts/moo.html

for Lunar Prospector:
http://lunar.arc.nasa.gov/

Because of the ever-changing nature of the Internet, we suggest that you preview all referenced Internet sites before allowing students to view them.

Vocabulary Activities

Introduce the following words and definitions.

astronaut a pilot or crew member of a spacecraft

axis a real or imaginary line through an object, such as a planet or moon, about which the object spins

comet a body in space made of frozen ice and dust that shines brightly and forms a long tail when it approaches the sun

crater a round pit or hollow shaped like a bowl on the surface of a heavenly body

eclipse a partial or complete darkening of one heavenly body by another when both line up with the sun or another star

Fahrenheit a scale for measuring temperature on which 32 degrees is the freezing point and 212 degrees is the boiling point of water

meteor a mass of rock or metal that enters the earth's atmosphere from space and usually burns up. A meteor that reaches the earth's surface is called a meteorite.

orbit the path that the moon travels around the earth or the earth travels around the sun

phase one of several appearances or stages of a thing, like the moon

solar system the sun and all the planets, moons, and other bodies that move around it

 You may wish to use the Vocabulary Master on page 57 to enhance students' understanding of the vocabulary words. These words and definitions are also listed in the Glossary on the last page of *On the Way to the Moon*.

Choose from among the following activities for additional practice with vocabulary.

Context Sentences Have students make up context sentences, using vocabulary words.

Word Web Encourage students to construct a word web with the word *moon* in the center.

Book Walk

Preview and Predict Tell students that *On the Way to the Moon* is nonfiction. It gives readers information about the moon. Direct students to examine the illustrations and photographs. Then ask: What do you think the book will tell you about why the moon looks different at different times?

Guide students to use the chapter titles on the Contents page to further predict what they expect to learn about the moon.

Strategy for Interactive Reading: Self-Assess

A good strategy for students to use as they read *On the Way to the Moon* is to assess themselves after they have completed each chapter. The Self-Assess Chart will serve as a source of questions, answers, and personal opinions about the book and will be useful as a review tool.

For each student, make a copy of the Self-Assess Strategic Reading Master on page 93 of this Teacher's Guide. Encourage students to use the chart as they progress from chapter to chapter.

You may wish to model how to fill in the chart for Chapter 1: **What did you learn?** *Early people made up stories about the moon and used it as a calendar.* **What was the best part?** *Some people thought the moon was a cat goddess.* **What questions do you still have?** *How did people begin to use the moon as a calendar?* **What could you do to answer your questions?** *Read the rest of the book or read another book about the moon.*

If students read the book **independently**, have them answer the questions after they read each chapter. For students who need more **teacher support**, help them answer the questions for another chapter.

Setting a Purpose for Reading

Before students begin reading *On the Way to the Moon*, ask them to read to find out what we know about the moon today and how we discovered what we know. Encourage students who are reading **independently** to stop periodically to set their own purpose for reading on.

For students who are reading with more **teacher support**, vary the ways in which you set a purpose for reading. For example, students might read further to find out what Galileo learned about the moon through his telescope.

More About...
The Moon

- The moon is the closest natural satellite to the sun. At one-third the earth's size, it is larger in comparison with its planet than any other satellite except Pluto's moon, Charon, which is just under one-half the size of the planet it orbits. Both the systems are known as double planets for this reason.

- As often happens with new scientific discoveries or theories, not everyone agrees with the finding of water ice on the moon. Astronaut Harrison Schmitt, the only geologist to walk on the moon, has said that it is too early to tell whether *Lunar Prospector* has discovered water ice. He points out that the probe cannot detect water ice directly. It can only detect the presence of hydrogen at the moon's polar areas, which it has. But this hydrogen could be part of the solar wind that has been caught in the cold traps at the poles.

Support All Learners

The following activities can be used during or after reading to address different learning levels and styles.

Easy
Encourage students to make up their own "first words" — words they would say if they were the first person on a space mission to reach some new place in the solar system. Have them choose what heavenly body they would visit, then tell what they would say.

Average
Have students create their own names for months. Suggest they look at a calendar and come up with a name for each month that describes events at that time of year that are important to them.

Challenging
Encourage students to think of an experiment or an activity they would want to perform if they traveled to the moon. Have them reread the relevant text portions and then describe their experiment in writing or show it with illustrations.

Addressing Multiple Intelligences

Verbal-Linguistic Learners
Have students work in small groups to write short dramatic pieces with characters from the myths they read about in Chapter 1. For example, one group might create a dramatic scene between the two brothers whom the Abaluyia people of Kenya believed represented the moon and the sun.

Logical-Mathematical Learners
Students may enjoy figuring out how much they would weigh on the moon. Have them use the numbers on page 15 to determine that the moon has about one sixth of the earth's gravity. Then have them divide their own weight by six to determine their "moon" weight. Provide assistance where needed.

Bodily-Kinesthetic Learners
Students may enjoy role-playing the physical conditions they would experience in certain moon-related situations. For example, they might mime walking or leaping as if they were on the moon.

English as a Second Language

Students whose native language is not English may enjoy sharing their own people's moon myths, along with the meaning of the moon in their own culture, with the rest of the class.

Help all students with the pronunciations of the difficult names in the text. Also encourage ESL learners to write brief descriptions of the various moon photos in the text. On the chalkboard, write verbs such as *wax, wane, bulge, rotate,* and so forth. Then pantomime the verbs as you point to each one. Have students copy your motions while saying the words.

During Reading

Independent Reading

For students who are reading **independently**, you may wish to make a quick check of comprehension at the midpoint and at the end of *On the Way to the Moon*, using these questions.

Midpoint

Comprehension Check
- Why did it take humans so long to solve some moon mysteries? *(Some questions could not be answered until humans had better telescopes.)* **Critical Response**
- What did scientists have to know about the moon before they could safely send people there? *(The moon's surface was not too hot and was flat enough to land on.)* **Critical Response**

End of Book

Comprehension Check
- Why is the possibility of ice on the moon an important discovery? *(Ice would provide water for people to use for living on the moon.)* **Critical Response**
- What kinds of activities would you enjoy doing if you lived in a colony on the moon? *(Answers will vary.)* **Creative Response**

Teacher-Supported Reading

For students who are reading with **teacher support**, use the chapter-by-chapter Comprehension Checks as a quick check of students' understanding. Teachable Moments are referenced to highlight points during reading at which you might wish to use a Skill Mini-Lesson. Reader Response questions are also provided. From time to time, you may wish to have students respond to these questions in writing.

Chapter 1 (pages 5–11)

Comprehension Check
- Why did early people make up stories about the moon? *(They did not have the technology to learn what the moon was really like.)* **Critical: Cause and Effect**
- In the sentence, "The ancient Egyptians connected the moon to a cat goddess named Bast," what parts of speech are the words *connected* and *named*? *(They are verbs.)* **Word Study: Inflected Forms**

Teachable Moment
To give students more practice with inflected forms, use the Word Study Skill Mini-Lesson on page 55.

Reader Response
- What parts or areas of the moon would you look for if you had a telescope? *(Answers will vary.)* **Creative: Personal Expression**

Chapter 2 (pages 12–16)

Comprehension Check
- How do you know that there is also day and night on the surface of the moon? *(The moon spins on its axis just as the earth does.)* **Critical: Drawing Conclusions**
- If you wanted to find the pronunciation of the word *basalt*, what resource would you use? *(a dictionary)* **Study Skills: Locating Sources of Information**

Teachable Moment
You may wish to use the Study Skills Mini-Lesson on Locating Sources of Information on page 54 of this Teacher's Guide.

Reader Response
- How would you study a moon rock if you could look at one? *(Responses will vary.)* **Creative: Personal Response**

ON THE WAY TO THE MOON—Nonfiction

ON THE WAY TO THE MOON

Chapter 3 (pages 17–24)

Comprehension Check
- Look at the diagram on page 20. What has to happen for there to be an eclipse of the sun? *(The moon has to be between the sun and the earth to block the sun's light.)* **Study Skills: Diagram**

Teachable Moment
You may wish to review the use of diagrams with the Study Skills Mini-Lesson: Using Graphic Aids–Diagram on page 54.

- Why does the temperature on the earth's surface drop during a solar eclipse? *(The sun's light is blocked.)* **Critical: Making Inferences**

Reader Response
- Why do you think early people were more frightened of solar eclipses than of lunar eclipses? *(Answers will vary.)* **Creative: Personal Response**

Chapter 4 (pages 25–29)

Comprehension Check
- What natural force makes it necessary for a spacecraft to have a powerful rocket to push it away from the earth? *(gravity)* **Critical: Drawing Conclusions**

- Read the material on page 26. Now complete this sentence: Gravity is to pull as rocket is to _____. *(push)* **Word Study: Analogies**

Teachable Moment *Skill Master*
To provide students with more practice with analogies, use the Word Study Mini-Lesson: Analogies on page 55 of this Teacher's Guide.

Reader Response
- Why do you think the Greeks made up a story of a man who tried to fly? *(Answers will vary.)* **Creative: Personal Opinion**

Chapter 5 (pages 30–34)

Comprehension Check
- Why did NASA continue to send instruments to the moon? *(to learn more about parts of the moon that hadn't been studied by the astronauts)* **Critical: Making Inferences**

- In connection with this book, what general name would you give to the group of things that includes craters, mountains, valleys, and flat lands? *(features of the moon's surface)* **Critical: Classify/Categorize**

Teachable Moment *Skill Master*
Students may benefit from learning more about classification in the Comprehension Skills Mini-Lesson: Classify/Categorize on page 53.

Reader Response
- What object or objects would you take to leave on the surface of the moon if you traveled there? Remember that whatever you choose must be lightweight. *(Answers will vary.)* **Creative: Personal Response**

Chapter 6 (pages 35–39)

Comprehension Check
- Why have scientists believed there is no water on the moon? *(Moon rocks they have studied have no water in them, and photographs of the moon's surface show no trace of running water.)* **Critical: Main Idea**

- Why did scientists consider the possibility that there might have been water on the moon at one time? *(They knew that pieces of comets, that contained ice, had crashed into the moon.)* **Critical: Making Judgments**

- Why do you think the author writes about the possibility of turning the moon's ice into water? *(The author wants to show readers that it may be possible for human beings to live for long periods of time on the moon.)* **Critical: Author's Purpose**

Reader Response
- How do you think moon ice could be used in the future? *(Answers will vary)* **Creative: Personal Response**

Chapter 7 (pages 40–47)

Comprehension Check
- What does it mean that the moon could become a "stepping stone" for exploring the solar system? *(The moon would be a place to stop before traveling further into the solar system.)* **Critical: Drawing Conclusions**
- The following sentence is another way to say the information on one page of Chapter 7: *The moon could be used as a springboard for space missions.* Which page is it? *(Page 44)* **Critical: Paraphrasing**

Teachable Moment
For more practice with paraphrasing, work with students to complete the Comprehension Skill Mini-Lesson: Paraphrasing on page 53.

Reader Response
- What do you think is the most important information that scientists have learned about the moon? *(Answers will vary.)* **Creative: Personal Response**

More — English as a Second Language

To help students understand descriptions of eclipses, orbits, and phases of the moon, you may wish to model these events using balls of different sizes and a lamp. Have students hold the balls and move them as you direct. Use words from the text to describe what happens. At first, use only single words and phrases, having students repeat after you. Then model the events again, this time using short, but complete sentences.

After Reading

Reader Response Activities

After students have completed *On the Way to the Moon*, you may wish to choose from the following activities.

Announcing a News Story

Have students write a short news story about the events of the first moon landing. They may use information from the text. Call on several volunteers to read their news stories to the class to see how each one approached the subject. **Writing/Speaking/Listening**

Writing a Journal Entry

Invite students to imagine they are one of the astronauts discussed in the text. Have them write a journal entry about their particular mission. Encourage them to include how they felt while awaiting takeoff, and whether they were scared, excited, hopeful. **Writing**

Drawing a Mythical Character

Encourage students to draw their own version of one of the mythical characters discussed in the text. After they have completed their artwork have them write a brief description of the mythical character. **Writing**

CURRICULUM CONNECTIONS

Art Activity
Making Spacecraft Models

Provide art materials for making spacecraft models, such as cardboard tubes, flat cardboard, small empty bottles for modules, colored construction paper, tape, glue, paints, colored pencils, and so on. Have students work individually, in pairs, or in small groups to make models of the spacecraft pictured in the text or of spacecraft of which they have found pictures elsewhere. Suggest students hang or display their completed models in the classroom.

Language Arts Activity
Creating a Myth

Invite students to choose something about the moon that they find interesting and make up a myth to explain it. Have them imagine they are someone in an early civilization who does not have scientific knowledge about the moon. Student myths can be funny, serious, scary—whatever students find useful in telling their stories.

Social Studies Activity
Making a Time Line

Have students use reference sources to find information about the dates of the six Apollo missions that landed on the moon. Have them create a time line and enter each mission, with start and finish dates, and, if room, the names of the three astronauts who completed each mission. A related Internet site is

http:\\lsda.ksc.nasa.gov/history/apollo.html

Science Research Activity
Tracking Moon Exploration and Information

For a month, have students keep their own notebook of things they learn in the newspaper, on television, or in books about recent moon discoveries. Have them describe each discovery or new fact, tell whether it changes our previous knowledge, and also tell what it may mean for the future of space exploration.

SKILL MINI-LESSONS

The following skill lessons may be used while or after students read the book *On the Way to the Moon*.

COMPREHENSION: Classify/Categorize

Objective: To group, or classify, things that are similar

Teach
Ask students what objects they would place into a group named "School Supplies." Students will probably suggest pencils, pens, paper, paints, books, and so forth. Point out to students that they have just used a skill called *classifying*. They put similar things into the same group, or class.

Practice
Have students reread the first paragraph on page 30. Encourage them to consider how the group of people named is similar. *(They are all astronauts; they all flew in Apollo 11; they all went to the moon.)* Encourage students to think of titles of the groups, or classes, into which they would put the three names. *(Examples: Astronauts; Apollo Astronauts; The First Astronauts to Go to the Moon)*

Evaluate
You may wish to use Comprehension Skill Master: Classify/Categorize on page 58 to evaluate students' understanding of the skill.

COMPREHENSION SKILL: Paraphrasing

Objective: To paraphrase or restate information

Teach
Direct students to their rewording of material from Chapter 7 to match it with the original text on page 44. Write the word *paraphrase* on the chalkboard and tell students it means to reword a section of text in a different way. Remind students that they paraphrase all the time. For example, a friend tells them a funny story at school. Later, at home, they retell the same story to their family, using their own words.

Impress on students that a good paraphrase must contain the same main ideas and basic information as the original, but be stated in different words.

Practice
Have students read page 42. Then have them determine which of the following is the best paraphrase of that material. Remind them that the paraphrase conveys the same basic ideas, but in different words.

People could live on the moon if they could use the oxygen in water to breathe and the hydrogen for growing plants.

The oxygen and hydrogen in the moon's water could be used for different things. Scientists could live on the moon.

Evaluate
Have volunteers justify their choice for the best paraphrase and tell why the others are not good examples.

STUDY SKILLS: Using Graphic Aids—Diagram

Objective: To read and interpret a diagram

Teach

Have students look at the diagram of the solar eclipse on page 20. Ask them to use the diagram to answer this question: What has to happen to the sun, earth, and moon in order for there to be an eclipse of the moon? *(The sun, earth, and moon all have to be in a straight line.)*

Explain that text is made clearer with the use of diagrams, such as the one on page 20. Point out the elements of a diagram.

- one or more objects in some kind of relationship
- labels that tell what the objects are (and sometimes the parts of an object) and what relationship is being diagrammed

Ask students what labels they see on this diagram. *(sun, earth, moon)*

Practice

Refer students to the description of the moon phases on page 18. Ask students what they would show on a diagram of the phases. Help students understand that they could show the earth in the middle and a circle around the earth to show the moon's orbit. Along the circle, they could draw and label the different phases: new moon, waxing moon, full moon, and waning moon.

STUDY SKILLS: Locating Sources of Information

Objective: To determine the best reference sources to use to find specific information

Teach

Remind students that in Chapter 2 they determined they would find the pronunciation of the word *basalt* in a dictionary. Point out that different kinds of reference sources can be used to find different types of information. For example

- an encyclopedia gives basic information about many subjects
- an atlas contains a variety of maps
- a biography tells about a person's life
- a dictionary contains word meanings, pronunciations, parts of speech, and usage suggestions
- a thesaurus contains synonyms and antonyms

Sometimes information can be found in more than one kind of source.

Practice

Direct students to the rest of the material in Chapter 2. Discuss where they would look to find the following information: the date and place of Galileo's birth; the history of the telescope; the plural of the word *axis*; the meaning of the word *reflect*; where and how the rock basalt is formed; whether *well-known* is a synonym for *famous*; where Neil Armstrong went to school.

Evaluate

Have students look through this chapter and Chapter 1 to find and list examples of things they would like to know more about. Ask them to list one or two sources in which they might find more information.

WORD STUDY: Analogies

Objective: To identify and create analogies

Teach

Recall with students the sentence they completed about gravity and a rocket. Write the complete sentence on the chalkboard—*Gravity* is to *pull* as *rocket* is to *push*. Tell students that the sentence is an analogy. It shows that the subjects in the first part of the sentence have the same relationship to one another as the subjects in the second part of the sentence. Gravity pulls down while a rocket pushes up.

Now write the following analogy on the chalkboard: *John Glenn* is to *American* as *Alexei Leonov* is to *Russian*. Ask students to identify the relationship in the two parts of the analogy.

Practice

Tell students that some analogies are simply a relationship between words and their definitions. Ask them to complete this analogy, based on the material in the last paragraph on page 18: *Wax* is to *bigger* as _____ is to _____. *(wane, smaller)* Other analogies are related to size. Have them complete this analogy, taken from the first paragraph on page 13: _____ is to *soccer ball* as _____ is to _____. *(Earth; moon, softball)*

Evaluate

You may wish to use Word Study Master: Analogies on page 59 to evaluate students' understanding of this skill.

WORD STUDY: Inflected Forms

Objective: To identify and use the *-s, -es, -ed,* and *-ing* forms of verbs

Teach

Recall with students the sentence in Chapter 1—*The ancient Egyptians connected the Moon to a cat goddess named Bast.* Students identified the words *connected* and *named* as verbs. Point out that the *-ed* ending makes the past tense of the verb. Point out that other endings for many verbs are *-s, -es,* and *-ing.* Write the following on the chalkboard

        to name
she names   we named   they are naming

Have students tell when each action happens: in the past, or in the present. Then call on volunteers to identify the ending of each verb.

Practice

Have students make a list of the following verbs taken from Chapter 1 and write the inflected forms next to each one: *live, believe, work, look.* Have them set up their paper to look like this:

explain   explains   explained   explaining

After they have made their inflected forms list, encourage them to use some of the different forms in sentences or in a paragraph.

Evaluate

Select other verbs from the book and have students tell which form is used, present or past, and how they know.

Home-School Connection

Dear Family,

Our class is reading chapter books that have to do with discoveries. The book we are reading currently is *On the Way to the Moon* by Becky Gold. It tells about the moon in terms of mythology, history, and discoveries made by scientists.

Discover Together

- You may want use the local library to help your child find out more about the moon. Here are some books to look for:

    The Moon by David Hughes (Facts on File, 1990)

    The Moon by Seymour Simon (Macmillan, 1984)

    The First Travel Guide to the Moon: What to Pack, How to Go, and What to See When You Get There by Rhoda Blumberg (Macmillan, 1984)

- Check your local video store for documentaries or movies about the moon, such as *Apollo 13*.

Conexión con el hogar

Estimada familia:

En este capítulo, nuestra clase está leyendo libros que están relacionados con descubrimientos. El libro que estamos leyendo en la actualidad se titula *On the Way to the Moon* de Becky Gold, que trata sobre la Luna en términos de mitología, historia y descubrimientos realizados por científicos.

Descubran juntos

- Pueden visitar la biblioteca local para ayudar a su hijo/a a aprender más acerca de la Luna. Estos son algunos de los libros que pueden buscar:

    The Moon de David Hughes (Facts on File, 1990)

    The Moon de Seymour Simon (Macmillian, 1984)

    The First Travel Guide to the Moon: What to Pack, How to Go, and What to See When You Get There de Rhoda Blumberg (Macmillan, 1984)

- Busquen en la tienda de vídeos local documentales o películas acerca de la Luna tales como *Apollo 13*.

Vocabulary Master

Name _____

 # Vocabulary: Glossary Words

Fill in each blank in the story with a word from the box.

orbit	phase	eclipse	comet	solar system
astronaut	meteor	Fahrenheit	axis	crater

I had a dream last night that I was an (1)_____ in space. My spaceship landed on the moon inside a (2) _____. I had to climb up to the rim! It was daylight, and it was boiling hot! It was over 200 degrees (3) _____.

The moon turned on its (4) _____ to make day and night, just like on Earth. It also traveled around Earth in an (5) _____. This path took about a month. I wondered which (6) _____ of the moon my friends were seeing on Earth.

Then one day, Earth moved between the moon and the sun. The shadow of the (7)_____ made it very dark for awhile.

One night I saw the bright tail of a (8)_____. I hoped a (9) _____ would not hit the moon. I'd really like to visit the whole (10) _____ and see all the planets. Maybe I will in my next dream!

ON THE WAY TO THE MOON—Nonfiction

SKILL MASTER

Name _____

Comprehension: Classify/Categorize

Write a group name from the box to classify each list of objects.

```
Inventions          Bodies in Space
People              Phases of the Moon
```

_____   _____

the Abaluyia   telescope

the Babylonians   rocket launcher

the Egyptians   spaceship

the Haida   probe

_____   _____

new moon   comet

waxing moon   earth

full moon   meteor

waning moon   moon

Write examples under each group name. You can use examples from the book or from your own knowledge.

Names from Myths   Scientists

_____   _____

_____   _____

_____   _____

SKILL MASTER

Name _____

Word Study: Analogies

An analogy compares two related words to another pair of words that are related in the same way.

Finish each analogy by filling in the circle next to the correct answer.

1. Pilot is to plane as astronaut is to _____.
   ○ train   ○ spacecraft   ○ bus

2. Foot is to length as Fahrenheit is to _____.
   ○ temperature   ○ mile   ○ weight

3. New moon is to dark as full moon is to _____.
   ○ dim   ○ colorful   ○ bright

4. Tides are to oceans as phases are to _____.
   ○ Mars   ○ moon   ○ sun

Choose a pair of words to complete each analogy. Write the words on the lines.

   telescope–stars   *Lunar Prospector*–spacecraft

5. *Titanic* is to ship as _____ is to _____.

6. Microscope is to cells as _____ is to _____.

ON THE WAY TO THE MOON—Nonfiction

THE LOST AND FOUND GAME

DISCOVERIES: BOOK 19

GENRE: FICTION

Summary

Jody and her friends, Brad, Tina, and Ben, are trying to find a way to raise money. They decide to have a rummage sale at the neighborhood street fair. When Jody's grandfather lets the kids help themselves to old stuff in his attic, they discover many treasures, including a mysterious box. Later that week, Jody's class visits the Quincy Museum where the kids make another discovery. Jody's grandfather's box is really an old Wari board, an ancient game from Africa. Jody's grandfather teaches them how to play. Then the kids have another idea: why not make Wari boards and sell them at the fair? Their homemade game boards are a huge success.

Home-School Connection

The Home-School activity master on page 72 of this Teacher's Guide provides a variety of activities students can do at home with family members.

PLANNER

SKILLS OVERVIEW
Use skills lessons before, during, or after reading.

Comprehension
Point of View
Character
Author's Purpose

Study Skills
Using Resources—Technology

Word Study
Prefixes
Compound Words

Strategic Reading
Visualizing—Character

Vocabulary
sponsor, p. 8
confused, p. 14
ancient, p. 16
museum, p. 17
donate, p. 18
attic, p. 25
gadgets, p. 26
exhibit, p. 30
valuable, p. 35
permission, p. 41

Activity/Skill Masters
Home-School Activity Master, p. 72
Vocabulary Master, p. 73
Comprehension Skill Master: Point of View, p. 74
Word Study Skill Master: Prefixes, p. 75
Strategic Reading Master: Visualizing, p. 95

For **theme-related projects**, see pages 9–11 of this Teacher's Guide.

THE LOST AND FOUND GAME—Fiction

Options for Using *The Lost and Found Game*

There are two ways in which you can use *The Lost and Found Game*. You may elect to have individuals, pairs, or small groups read independently, or you may wish to guide the instruction of each chapter more closely. Use the suggestions under **INDEPENDENT READING** with individuals, pairs, or small groups who can read the book independently. For students who need more instructional guidance, use the suggestions under **TEACHER-SUPPORTED READING**. Throughout the lesson plan, the words **independently** and **teacher support** appear in boldface type for easy identification.

Independent Reading	Teacher-Supported Reading

Before Reading
• Build Background (p. 62)
  Internet Activity
• Vocabulary Activities (p. 62)
  Vocabulary Master (p. 73)
• Book Walk (p. 63)
• Strategic Reading Master:
  Visualizing—Character (p. 95)
	Before Reading
	• Build Background (p. 62)
	  Internet Activity
	• Vocabulary Activities (p. 62)
	  Vocabulary Master (p. 73)
	• Book Walk (p. 63)
	• Strategic Reading Master:
	  Visualizing—Character (p. 95)

During Reading • Setting a Purpose for Reading (p. 63)	**During Reading** • Support All Learners—Choose from among the activities for learners of varying abilities, for multiple intelligences, and for English as a second language. (p. 64) • Setting a Purpose for Reading (p. 63) • Chapter-by-Chapter Comprehension Checks (pp. 65–67)

After Reading
• Support All Learners—You may wish to have students do the challenging activity or any of the activities under Addressing Multiple Intelligences. (p. 64)
• Reader Response Activities (p. 68)
  Writing Directions
  Creating an Ad
• Curriculum Connections (p. 68)
  Playing Wari
  Searching for a Museum
• Skill Mini-Lessons (pp. 69–71)
  Skill Masters (pp. 74–75)
	After Reading
	• Reader Response Activities (p. 68)
	• Curriculum Connections (p. 68)
	• Skill Mini-Lessons (pp. 69–71)
	  Skill Masters (pp. 74–75)

Before Reading

Build Background

Ask students if they have ever bought something at a rummage sale. Explain that people often have these kinds of sales in order to raise money, and also to clean out the garage or basement! (Other names for this kind of sale include garage sale, attic sale, or tag sale.) Have students describe the kinds of things one might find for sale there.

Tell students that sometimes old toys and games are sold at rummage sales. Elicit the names of common board games. You may wish to have students working **independently** complete a chart such as the one below for common games. Assist students who need more **teacher support**.

Name of Game	Number of Players	Type of Board
Checkers	2	Checkerboard

Internet Interested students may wish to find out more about games by using the following Internet addresses.

www.kidsdomain.com/games/online1.html

www.funbrain.com/

Because of the ever-changing nature of the Internet, we suggest that you preview all referenced Internet sites before allowing students to view them.

Vocabulary Activities

Introduce the following words and definitions.

ancient of great age; very old

attic a space in a house that is just below the roof and above the other rooms

confused mixed up

donate to make a gift of

exhibit things shown publicly

gadgets small tools made to do a certain job

museum a building or room where a collection of objects is kept and displayed

permission the act of letting someone do something

sponsor a person or group who helps another person or group by paying expenses

valuable having great worth

 You may wish to use the Vocabulary Skill Master on page 73 to enhance students' understanding of the vocabulary words. These words and definitions are also listed in the Glossary on the last page of *The Lost and Found Game*.

Choose from among the following activities for additional practice with vocabulary.

Illustrated Words Invite students to draw a picture that contains illustrations of as many of the vocabulary words as possible. Have them label the words as they appear in the drawing.

Word Search Distribute graph paper and invite students to work with a partner to create a word-search puzzle using the vocabulary words. Suggest they list the words beneath the puzzle.

Context Paragraph Have students write a paragraph that uses as many of the vocabulary words as possible.

Book Walk

Preview and Predict Have students examine the cover and the illustrations in *The Lost and Found Game*. Do they recognize the characters from previous books? Based on the illustrations and the title, what do they think the book will be about?

Next, have students examine the Contents page of *The Lost and Found Game* and read the chapter titles. Then ask: What kind of game do you think is involved? What do you think will happen in the story?

Strategy for Interactive Reading: Visualizing—Character

Recall with students the names of the characters (whom they have met in previous books). Explain that a good strategy for students to use as they read *The Lost and Found Game* is to visualize the characters as they read.

Make a copy for each student of the Strategic Reading Master: Visualizing Character, on page 95 of this Teacher's Guide. Introduce the strategy, explaining that the chart will help students think about the differences between the characters in this story.

Encourage students to make notes about the characters as they read the story. For students who are reading *The Lost and Found Game* **independently**, have them fill in the strategy master as they read. With students who need more **teacher support**, you may refer to the strategy master from time to time, as you read the book together.

Setting a Purpose for Reading

Have students read aloud the title of the first chapter of *The Lost and Found Game*. Encourage students to speculate about the title of the book and the title of this chapter. Suggest students read the first chapter to find out what the book is about. For students who are reading **independently**, suggest that at the end of each chapter they ask themselves a question about what will happen next in the story.

For students who are reading with more **teacher support**, give guidance in formulating questions at the end of each chapter. Stop periodically to help students apply information learned about the characters to complete the graphic organizer.

More About...
Games

- Chess is one of the oldest and the most widely played games in the world. It is based on a game that began in northern India in the fifth century. Originally, chess was played with four players.

- Backgammon is even older than Chess. It began as a dice and board game in ancient Ur about 3000 B.C. The Romans played a similar game.

- Baseball developed from an English game called rounders in the 1700's. The first organized game of baseball was played in Hoboken, New Jersey, on June 17, 1846.

- *Wari* is a version of a more familiar game called *Mancala*. *Mancala* is played with the addition of a cup on each side of the board where players put the stones they collect.

Support All Learners

The following activities can be used during or after reading to address different learning levels and styles.

Easy
Have students write a sentence that summarizes what plot event happens in each chapter. You may wish to do this together, writing each statement on the chalkboard to create a sequence chart.

Average *(Portfolio)*
Have students figure out how much time elapses in this story by having them make a chart for the days of the week, and note what the kids do on each day. Tell them they will have to read ahead to Chapter 4 before they learn what day of the week it is then work backward from that day.

Challenging
Provide students with egg cartons and beans. Suggest they work in pairs to read the directions on the inside back cover of the book to learn how to play Wari.

Addressing Multiple Intelligences

Verbal-Linguistic Learners *(Portfolio)*
Have students write out the directions for playing a simple game. Have other students, who don't already know the game, follow the directions to learn to play.

Bodily-Kinesthetic Learners
Suggest students outline a large Wari board on the playground with chalk, and use beanbags to play.

Logical-Mathematical Learners
Brad thought at first that the Wari board was a counting device, like an abacus. Suggest students figure a way to use an egg carton to make a counting device. (If they work with base 10, they will have to cut off two sections of the carton.)

Musical Learners
Many games involve songs or chants, such as jump rope rhymes. Have students learn or invent a song or chant that is part of playing a game.

English as a Second Language

Students acquiring English may benefit from a review of the skill of using context clues to figure out the meaning of new words. Explain that an author sometimes defines a word directly. Call students' attention to page 14, paragraph 5. Have them find the sentence in which Mrs. Martin explains the meaning of *rummage* and read her explanation aloud.

Explain to students that they can often figure out the meaning of a word even when the author does not define it directly. Call attention to the word *donate* on page 18. Help them use what they know to figure out that *donate* means *give*.

During Reading

Independent Reading

For students who are reading **independently**, you may wish to make a quick check of comprehension at the midpoint and at the end of *The Lost and Found Game*, using these questions.

Midpoint

Comprehension Check
- What problem are the children trying to solve? *(They want to raise money for new baseball uniforms.)* **Critical Response**
- What do you think the mysterious box will turn out to be? *(Answers will vary.)* **Creative Response**

End of Book

Comprehension Check
- What was the box from Jody's grandfather's attic? *(It was a game board for Wari, an African game.)* **Critical Response**
- Do you think you'd like to try playing Wari? *(Answers will vary.)* **Creative Response**

Teacher-Supported Reading

For students who are reading with **teacher support**, use the chapter-by-chapter Comprehension Checks as a quick check of students' understanding. Teachable Moments are referenced to highlight points during reading at which you might wish to use a Skill Mini-Lesson. Reader Response questions are also provided. From time to time, you may wish to have students respond to these questions in writing.

Chapter 1 (pages 5–9)

Comprehension Check
- You know that in every story the characters have a problem to solve. What is the problem so far? *(The Little League team needs to get money for new uniforms.)* **Critical: Plot**
- Is Jody telling this story? How can you tell? *(No, it is told by an outside storyteller. The storyteller does not say "I.")* **Critical: Point of View**

Teachable Moment *Skill Master*
You may want to use the Comprehension Skill Mini-Lesson on Point of View at this time. It is found on page 69 of this guide.

Reader Response
- What would you do about uniforms if you were a member of the Little League team? *(Answers will vary.)* **Creative: Personal Reaction**

Chapter 2 (pages 10–15)

Comprehension Check
- What does the fact that Jody noticed the banner advertising the street fair tell you about her character? *(Jody is alert and notices things.)* **Critical: Character**

Teachable Moment
You might wish to use the Comprehension Skill Mini-Lesson on Character with students at this time. It is on page 69 of this guide.

- What important idea does the banner give Jody's mother? *(She suggests that the kids have a rummage sale at the fair.)* **Critical: Plot**

Reader Response
- Have you ever been to a rummage sale? Describe what it was like. *(Answers will vary.)* **Creative: Personal Response**

Chapter 3 (pages 16–22)

Comprehension Check
- What can you tell about Brad based on the information in this chapter? *(He is smart. He is a good student.)* **Critical: Character**
- Why did the kids make a sign? *(They needed to collect things to sell, so they made a sign to advertise.)* **Critical: Cause/Effect**

Reader Response
- What else might the kids do to advertise for their rummage sale? *(Answers will vary.)* **Creative: Personal Response**

Chapter 4 (pages 23–29)

Comprehension Check
- What is the mystery box that the chapter title refers to? *(It is the narrow box that Jody found in her grandfather's attic.)* **Critical: Main Idea**
- Reread page 25. What word does Jody's grandfather use to describe his attic? What does it mean? *(disordered; it means "not ordered", or "not in order".)* **Word Study: Prefixes**

Teachable Moment *Skill Master*
You may wish to use the Word Study Skill Mini-Lesson on prefixes at this time. You will find it on page 71 of this Teacher's Guide.

Reader Response
- What do you think the mystery box is? *(Answers will vary.)* **Creative: Expressing Opinions**

Chapter 5 (pages 30–40)

Comprehension Check
- What exciting discovery do the kids make at the museum? *(They see a game board that looks like their mystery box.)* **Critical: Main Idea**
- If you wanted to find the latest information about exhibits at a museum, what technology could you use to find out? *(You could telephone, look it up in a newspaper, or use the Internet.)* **Study Skills: Using Resources—Technology**

Teachable Moment
At this time you may want to use the Study Skills Mini-Lesson on Using Resources—Technology on page 70 of this Teacher's Guide.

Reader Response
- Reread the last sentence of this chapter. What do you think it means? *(Answers will vary.)* **Creative: Expressing Opinions**

Chapter 6 (pages 41–46)

Comprehension Check
- How were the egg cartons that Ben checked like the Wari board? *(They had six spaces on each side.)* **Critical: Making Comparisons**
- Do you think Ben's idea to make Wari boards out of egg cartons is a good one? Why or why not? *(Answers will vary, but students will probably agree that it is a good idea since the kids in their class were so interested in Jody's grandfather's game.)* **Critical: Making Judgments**

Reader Response
- If you were Ben's classmate, would you want one of his Wari boards? Why or why not? *(Answers will vary.)* **Creative: Personal Response**

Chapter 7 (pages 47–55)

Comprehension Check
- What kind of a person was Jody? How do you know? *(The author tells us she liked to think things through.)* **Critical: Character**
- On page 51 there is a compound word that describes the Wari board that Jody made. What is that word? *(homemade)* **Word Study: Compound Words**

Teachable Moment
You may find this a good time to review compound words. The Word Study Skill Mini-Lesson on Compound Words is on page 71 of this Teacher's Guide.

Reader Response
- Do you think the kids will raise enough money at the fair to buy uniforms? Why or why not? *(Answers will vary.)* **Creative: Expressing Opinions**

Chapter 8 (pages 56–63)

Comprehension Check
- Were the Wari boards a popular item? How can you tell? *(Yes, because they sold out and the kids took orders to make more.)* **Critical: Drawing Conclusions**
- Why do you think the author put the directions for Wari in the book? *(so that readers could learn how to play the game)* **Critical: Author's Purpose**

Teachable Moment
You may wish to use the Comprehension Skill Mini-Lesson on Author's Purpose at this time. You will find it on page 70 of this Teacher's Guide.

Reader Response
- What is your opinion of Wari? *(Answers will vary.)* **Creative: Expressing Opinions**

More: English as a Second Language

Students who are acquiring English may benefit from reviewing synonyms. Explain that there are many words in English that mean the same, or almost the same thing. For instance, in this story the synonyms *rummage* and *stuff* are used.

You may also wish to give special attention to words with more than one meaning, such as *store*, *fair*, and *sign*.

After Reading

Reader Response Activities

After students have completed *The Lost and Found Game*, you may wish to choose from the following activities.

Writing Directions

Ask students to choose a game that they know well, and write directions for it. Suggest that they have someone who does not play the game read and follow the directions to learn it. **Writing**

Making Museum Exhibits

Encourage students who collect things to bring them to class to make an exhibit. Have them write a label for each object. When they are ready, have students take turns describing their collections and reading the labels. **Writing/Speaking**

Creating an Ad

Have students work in small groups to create a commercial for a local event. Remind them that the commercial must include what is happening, and the time and place of the event. Allow them time to practice their skits and then share them with the class. **Speaking/Listening**

CURRICULUM CONNECTIONS

Social Studies Activity
Making a Classroom Museum

Invite students to work together to make a classroom display on a particular theme. For instance, students may enjoy bringing in the oldest object they have. Have them make a label telling the age and the use of the object.

Language Arts Activity
Playing Wari

Have students read and follow the directions to play Wari. You may wish to set up a round robin match or have students teach another class to play after they have mastered the game.

Mathematics Activity
Holding a Rummage Sale

Arrange for interested students to hold their own rummage sale at school to raise money for a class activity or special class purchase. Have them price the items, hold the sale, make change, and figure their profits.

Computer Research Activity
Searching for a Museum

Invite students to use the Internet to help compile a booklet showing interesting museums that are in your local area. Have them note the type of museum and any special exhibits, as well as the museum's hours and cost of admission. Have them write out directions to the museum, too. A related Internet site that students might be interested in is

www.vol.it/UK/EN/ARTE/MuseumsfromAtoZ.html

The following skill lessons may be used while or after students read *The Lost and Found Game*.

COMPREHENSION: Point of View

Objective: To understand the point of view of a story

Teach

Call students' attention to the opening sentences of *The Lost and Found Game*. Then ask students whether one of the characters is telling the story or whether there is an outside storyteller. Elicit that the story is told by a storyteller or narrator.

Write the following on the chalkboard: *Ben and I joined the team on the field.*

Challenge students to tell who is telling the story now. (*Jody*) Recall that when the storyteller uses *I* and is one of the characters in the story, this is called first-person point of view. When the story is told by an outside storyteller that uses *he, she, they*, this is called third-person point of view.

Practice

Have students read the first paragraph of *The Day the Sky Turned Green* from Set 1 of *First Chapters*. Encourage them to tell from whose point of view the story is told. (*First person—Champ's point of view.*)

Evaluate

Use the Comprehension Skill Master: Point of View on page 74 to evaluate students' understanding of this skill.

COMPREHENSION: Character

Objective: To understand how an author gives information about a character

Teach

Ask students to reread page 17. Remind students that one way readers learn about a story character is by what the character does or says. Ask students what they can tell about Brad from the information on this page. Elicit that he is smart and a good student. Point out that we know this from the way Brad answered Ms. Ramos's question, and also because the author tells us, "He always knew the answers."

Explain to students that other ways readers learn about story characters are by noting what other characters say about them, from information that the author gives, and from what the characters themselves do and say.

Practice

Have students reread page 6, then ask: What does Ben say to Brad? (*I know you're a great ball player, but I don't think you can read and play baseball at the same time!*) What do we learn about Brad from this? (*He is a good ball player and he likes to read.*) What do we learn about Ben? (*He likes to tease.*)

Evaluate

Encourage students to look for other places in the story where the author gives information about the characters, either directly, or by what the characters say and do.

COMPREHENSION: Author's Purpose

Objective: To understand an author's purpose for writing

Teach

Recall with students that there are three main purposes authors have for writing: to inform readers, to entertain readers, or to convince or persuade readers to think or act a certain way. Discuss different kinds of writing. Then ask students what they think was the author's purpose in writing *The Lost and Found Game*. Point out that to entertain might mean to make readers laugh, to surprise them, or even to scare them! Then call students' attention to the game directions for Wari on the inside back cover. Discuss with students why an author would include game directions in a fictional story.

Point out that an author can have more than one purpose. For instance, a book may entertain and give information, such as how to do something, at the same time.

Practice

Discuss the following types of writing and ask students to tell what they think the author's purpose is: a joke book *(entertain)*, an advertisement *(persuade)* a poster telling about a rummage sale *(inform, persuade)*, a cookbook *(to inform about how to do something)*.

Evaluate

Discuss other books students have read, and ask them to tell what they think the author's purpose was for writing them.

STUDY SKILLS: Using Resources—Technology

Objective: To become acquainted with some types of technology used for research

Teach

Display a CD-ROM version of an encyclopedia or dictionary. Tell students that there are many kinds of technology available to help them find information. With students' help, list and discuss the following.

- CD-ROM versions of encyclopedias and atlases are widely available.
- Many computers have dictionaries already installed. A dictionary gives definitions and pronunciations of words.
- Most libraries have the list of books they own on a computer catalog.
- The Internet has the latest, most up-to-date information on a vast amount of topics. To find information on the Internet, use a search engine such as AltaVista or WebCrawler.
- Although it has been around for almost a century, the telephone is still a wonderful invention for finding information!

Practice

Give students time to practice using whatever classroom technology is available, such as CD-ROM encyclopedias or the Internet. Arrange a visit to the school library or media center for a demonstration of the Internet.

Evaluate

Ask students to make a list of all the resources they can think of that would provide information about museums.

WORD STUDY: Prefixes

Objective: To understand prefixes

Teach

Write the word *disordered* on the chalkboard and remind students that this is what Jody's grandfather said about his attic. Ask students to tell what the word means. Point out the prefix *dis*, and explain that it means "not." Next, review with students other prefixes that mean not: *in-, un-*. Then write the following sentence on the chalkboard:

I reread my favorite parts of the book.

Ask students to identify the word with a prefix. Elicit that *re-* means to do again, so *reread* means "to read again."

Practice

Write the following words on the chalkboard: *regrouped, rewrote, rejoined, reboard, recheck, inexpensive, discontinue.* Have students circle each prefix, tell what the word means, and use it in a sentence.

Evaluate

You may wish to use the Word Study Skill Master: Prefixes to evaluate students' understanding of this skill.

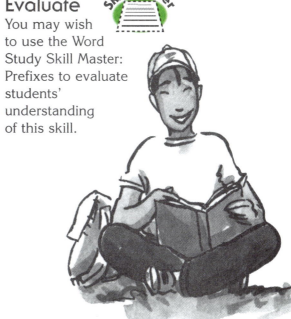

WORD STUDY: Compound Words

Objective: To identify compound words

Teach

Write the words *backpack, baseball,* and *schoolyard* on the chalkboard. Recall with students that these words are compound words, words that are made of two or more words that are written together. Call on volunteers to come to the board and underline each word that makes up the compound word. Explain that it is helpful to recognize compound words because the meaning of the word as a whole is related to the meaning of the two smaller words.

Practice

Write the following words on index cards and distribute them randomly: *pack, mates, ball, walk, board, out.* Then write the following words on the chalkboard.

back	team
base	side
poster	dug

Have students match a word on a card with a word on the chalkboard to make compound words. Have them use the word in a sentence to show what it means.

Evaluate

As students read other books, have them point out compound words.

Home-School Connection

Dear Family,

Our class is reading chapter books about discoveries. The book we are currently reading is *The Lost and Found Game* by Judy Nayer. In this book, a group of children discover an old game.

Discover Together

- You may want to go to the local library to help your child find information about games. Here are some books to look for.
    The Book of Classic Board Games by Sid Sackson (Klutz Press, 1991)
    The Games Treasury by Merilyn Simondo Mohr (Chapters Publishing, 1993)
- Get a classic board game such as backgammon or Parcheesi and play it with your child.
- Think of a game you may have played as a child, such as jacks, hopscotch, or jump rope. Does your child know the game? Have your child compare it to games he or she plays with friends.

Conexión con el hogar

Estimada familia:

En este capítulo, nuestra clase está leyendo libros que están relacionados con descubrimientos. El libro que estamos leyendo en la actualidad se titula *The Lost and Found Game* de Judy Nayer, en el cual un grupo de niños descubre un viejo tablero de juego. Ellos también descubren cómo usar este juego de mesa para reunir el dinero que necesitan para comprar nuevos uniformes deportivos.

Descubran juntos

- Pueden visitar la biblioteca local para ayudar a su hijo/a a encontrar más información acerca de juegos de mesa, incluyendo aquellos de otras culturas. Estos son algunos de los libros que pueden buscar:
    The Book of Classic Board Games de Sid Sackson (Klutz Press, 1991)
    The Games Treasury de Merilyn Simondo Mohr (Chapters Publishing, 1993)
- Consigan un juego de mesa clásico tal como *Backgammon* o *Parcheesi* y jueguen con su hijo/a.
- Piensen en un juego de su infancia: *jacks*, rayuela o saltar la cuerda. ¿Conocen este juego su hijo/a? ¿Lo han comparado su hijo/a a otros juegos que practican con sus amigos?

THE LOST AND FOUND GAME—Fiction

VOCABULARY MASTER

Name _____

Vocabulary: Glossary Words

Write a word from the box on each line to answer the question.

| attic | permission | valuable | ancient | donate |
| confused | museum | exhibit | gadgets | sponsor |

1. What do you give someone so they can do something?
   _____

2. What are small tools made for a certain job called?
   _____

3. Where might a collection of objects be displayed?
   _____

4. If something has great worth, what is it?
   _____

5. What is the space in a house just below the roof called?
   _____

6. What word describes making a gift of something?
   _____

7. What can you call something very old?
   _____

8. What word describes someone who is mixed up?
   _____

9. What is a display called where things are shown publicly?
   _____

10. What do we call someone who pays expenses for another person? _____

THE LOST AND FOUND GAME—Fiction

SKILL MASTER

Name _____

Comprehension: Point of View

A story can be told as if one of the characters in the story is telling it. This is called first-person point of view. In first person, the storyteller uses the words **I**, **me**, and **we**. A story can also be told by an outside storyteller. This is called third-person point of view.

Read the story beginnings below. Write **first person** or **third person** to show the point of view.

1. When my brother Joey was five years old and I was seven, a funny thing happened to us.

   _____

2. Long ago, when the earth was very young, there lived a very smart princess. She lived in a great stone castle with her mother, the queen, who ruled the land.

   _____

3. The Sixth Street Club members had all agreed to meet to discuss the problem. All the kids were really upset, and no one knew what to do. Each was hoping the others would have a solution.

   _____

4. My cat, Nicky, thinks he is part of the family. Whenever we sit at the table to eat dinner, Nicky meows that he wants to eat, too.

   _____

SKILLS MASTER

Name _____

 # Word Study Skill: Prefixes

Prefixes are word parts that are added to the beginnings of base words. Prefixes change the meaning of base words.

un-, in-, im-, dis-   mean "not, or the opposite of"

re-   means "again"

Read the sentences. Fill in the circle before the correct word.

1. Joe liked the story so much that he _____ it.
   ○ unread   ○ disread   ○ reread

2. We dug where the map said to dig, and we finally _____ a large wooden box.
   ○ recovered   ○ uncovered   ○ covered

3. We planned to buy only one, but we bought two CDs because they were really _____.
   ○ expensive   ○ disexpensive   ○ inexpensive

4. Jenny left the group when we got to the mall, but she _____ us an hour later.
   ○ rejoined   ○ disjoined   ○ joined

5. To fool us, Juan wrote his note in _____ ink.
   ○ visible   ○ revisible   ○ invisible

THE LOST AND FOUND GAME—Fiction   75

DISCOVERIES: BOOK 20
SECRETS OF THE RAIN FOREST
GENRE: NONFICTION

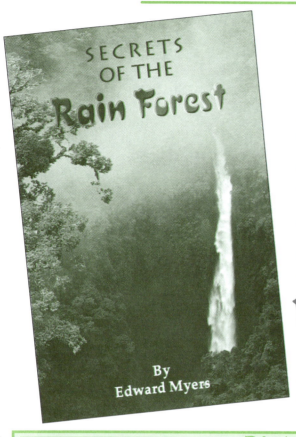

Summary

Secrets of the Rain Forest takes readers to one of the earth's premier ecosystems—the rain forests of the tropics. In a band around the earth at or near the equator lie hot, humid regions full of trees, vegetation, animals, and people not found anywhere else on the planet. The diversity of life found in such regions is threatened by human development, including logging, mining, ranching, and the habits of consumers in areas far from the rain forests themselves. This book shows readers some of the wonders of the South American rain forest and explains why it is important for people everywhere to help preserve it.

Home-School Connection

The Home-School activity master on page 88 of this Teacher's Guide provides a variety of activities students can do at home with family members.

PLANNER

SKILLS OVERVIEW
Use skill lessons before, during, or after reading.

Comprehension
Main Idea and Details
Drawing Conclusions

Study Skills
Using Graphic Aids—Maps
SQ3R

Word Study
Specialized Vocabulary
Multiple-Meaning Words

Strategic Reading
Synthesize Information

Vocabulary
climate, p. 5
ecosystem, p. 8
pollute, p. 15
atmosphere, p. 15
recent, p. 20
poisonous, p. 28
camouflage, p. 29
deforestation, p. 42
renewable, p. 45
recycle, p. 46

Activity/Skill Masters
Home-School Activity Master, p. 88
Vocabulary Master, p. 89
Comprehension Skill Master: Main Idea and Details, p. 90
Word Study Skill Master: Multiple-Meaning Words, p. 91
Strategic Reading Master: Synthesize Information, p. 96

For **theme-related projects**, see pages 10–11 of this Teacher's Guide.

SECRETS OF THE RAIN FOREST—Nonfiction

Options for Using *Secrets of the Rain Forest*

There are two ways in which you can use *Secrets of the Rain Forest*. You may elect to have individuals, pairs, or small groups read independently, or you may wish to guide the instruction of each chapter more closely. Use the suggestions under **INDEPENDENT READING** with individuals, pairs, or small groups who can read the book independently. For students who need more instructional guidance, use the suggestions under **TEACHER-SUPPORTED READING**. Throughout the lesson plan, the words **independently** and **teacher support** appear in boldface type for easy identification.

Independent Reading

Before Reading
- Build Background (p. 78)
  Internet Activity
- Vocabulary Activities (p. 78)
- Book Walk (p. 79)
- Strategic Reading Master:
  Synthesize Information (p. 96)

During Reading
- Setting a Purpose for Reading (p. 79)

After Reading
- Support All Learners—You may wish to have students do the challenging activity or any of the activities under Addressing Multiple Intelligences. (p. 80)
- Reader Response Activities (p. 84)
  Writing a News Article
- Curriculum Connections (p. 84)
  Tracing the Amazon River
  Figuring Out How Much Rain Forest Remains
  Researching a Rain-Forest People
- Skill Mini-Lessons (pp. 85–87)
  Skill Masters (pp. 90–91)

Teacher-Supported Reading

Before Reading
- Build Background (p. 78)
  Internet Activity
- Vocabulary Activities (p. 78)
- Book Walk (p. 79)
- Strategic Reading Master:
  Synthesize Information (p. 96)

During Reading
- Support All Learners—Choose from among the activities for learners of varying abilities, for multiple intelligences, and for English as a second language. (p. 80)
- Setting a Purpose for Reading (p. 79)
- Chapter-by-Chapter Comprehension Checks (pp. 81–83)

After Reading
- Reader Response Activities (p. 84)
- Curriculum Connections (p. 84)
- Skills Mini-Lessons (pp. 85–87)
  Skill Masters (pp. 90–91)

SECRETS OF THE RAIN FOREST—Nonfiction

Before Reading

Build Background

Invite students to tell what they know about rain forests from books, television, and movies. Where are rain forests found? Are there any tropical rain forests in the United States? Who lives in rain forests? What kinds of animals and plants are found there? Have students help you organize a chart like the one below, entering specific information under each heading. Students who are reading **independently** may add to their chart as they read. Allow students who need more **support** to suggest additional headings and entries to add to the chart as you read with them.

Rain Forests		
Where They Are Found	Why They Are Important	Living Things

Internet Interested students may wish to find out more about rain forests by using the following Internet addresses:

www.ran.org/kids_action/index.html

www.schools.ash.org.au/schools/rochedale/rain2/html

• Because of the ever-changing nature of the Internet, we suggest that you preview all referenced Internet sites before allowing students to view them.

Vocabulary Activities

Introduce the following words and definitions.

atmosphere the layer of gases that surrounds Earth, or all the air around Earth

camouflage anything, such as color or shape, that is used as a disguise in nature or to hide something

climate the average weather conditions of a place over many years

deforestation the removing of trees or forests from a piece of land

ecosystem an area in which living and nonliving things interact

poisonous capable of harming or killing by poison

pollute to make unclean

recent happened lately

recycle to use again and again, or to change to a new use

renewable able to be used or made again

 You may wish to use the Vocabulary Master on page 89 to enhance students' understanding of the vocabulary words. These words and definitions are also listed in the Glossary on the last page of *Secrets of the Rain Forest*.

Choose from among the following activities for additional practice with vocabulary.

Context Sentences Have students make up context sentences using as many of the vocabulary words as possible.

Word Web Invite students to make a word web focusing on the words *rain forest*. Suggest that they use as many of the vocabulary words as possible as well as words from *Secrets of the Rain Forest* to complete the web.

SECRETS OF THE RAIN FOREST—Nonfiction

Book Walk

Preview and Predict Tell students that *Secrets of the Rain Forest* is nonfiction. It presents information about the rain forests, their inhabitants, and their value to all living things on the earth.

Invite students to look at the photographs and to read the chapter titles on the Contents page. Ask the following questions: What kinds of information do you expect to learn from *Secrets of the Rain Forest*? What questions would you like answered?

Strategy for Interactive Reading: Synthesize Information

A good strategy for students to use as they read *Secrets of the Rain Forest* is to synthesize the important information they learn as they read.

Make a copy for each student of the Strategic Reading Master: Synthesizing Information, on page 96 of this Teacher's Guide. Have students write the word *rain forests* in the blank next to *Topic*. Explain that to synthesize information is to put facts together in a way that makes sense. Model an example of how to fill in the flowchart for Chapter 1 of *Secrets of the Rain Forest*. Remind students that they can gather information from the text, from charts, maps, or graphs, and from illustrations. They can then add new ideas of their own after they have read each chapter.

If students are reading *Secrets of the Rain Forest* **independently**, have them record their information on the flowchart. Help students who need more **teacher support** use the chapter titles, the graphics, and the illustrations as a focus and guide them to locate important ideas in each chapter.

Setting a Purpose for Reading

Before students begin reading *Secrets of the Rain Forest*, ask them to read to find out more about what rain forests mean to the animals, plants, and people who live there. Encourage students who are reading **independently** to stop periodically to set their own purpose for reading on. For students who are reading with more **teacher support**, vary the ways in which you set a purpose for reading. For example, students might read further to learn about the animals they see in the illustrations or to see what kinds of pollution threaten the rain forest.

More About...
The Rain Forest

- The largest rain forest on the earth is in South America, along the Amazon River system. The forest lies on much of the northern half of the continent in a region about two-thirds the size of the United States. It covers large parts of six countries — Brazil, Bolivia, Peru, Ecuador, Colombia, and Venezuela.

- The Amazon River is the largest, though not the longest, river in the world, with over 1,000 tributaries. It carries two-thirds of all the fresh water on the earth. At certain points, the river is too wide for a person to see from shore to shore, as though it were a vast inland ocean.

SECRETS OF THE RAIN FOREST—Nonfiction

Support All Learners

The following activities can be used during or after reading to address different learning levels and styles.

Easy
Have students draw or paint their own illustrations of interesting animals or plants they read about in the book. They can label their illustrations and write a brief description of what they have drawn.

Average
Have students write their own captions for some of the photographs in the text. Encourage them to be specific about color, size, movement, surroundings, and so forth.

Challenging
Invite students to classify the animals they read about into groups such as mammals, birds, reptiles, amphibians, and so on.

Addressing Multiple Intelligences

Interpersonal Learners
Encourage students who enjoy debate and argument to make notes so that they can persuade someone of the value of the rain forest. Encourage students to use colorful words to describe the rain forest and opinion phrases such as "I believe," "I think," "I feel," and so on. If possible, allow students to hold a debate.

Naturalistic Learners
Encourage students to create a poster that shows one or more of the following features of *Secrets of the Rain Forest*: animals, plants, people of the rain forest, threats to the rain forest, how to save the rain forest. The posters should contain graphics as well as punched-up words and phrases. When they are finished, display the posters around the classroom.

Musical Learners
Invite interested students to write a song about the rain forest. They can use a melody from a song they already know, or make up one of their own. Some students might wish to work on the music while others write the words. Have students perform their song for the rest of the class.

English as a Second Language

Students acquiring English who come from regions where there are rain forests, such as Central America, South America, and Asia, might like to give the names for some of the species in the book in their native languages. Write the words on the board next to the animal or plant name in English.

Be sure that students understand how to pronounce the unfamiliar words, both those with given pronunciations and those without. Also have students note the different kinds of descriptions in the text — "a deer the size of a rabbit," "a frog that flies," "[vines that] look like ropes dangling from tall trees...", as well as colorful verbs such as *curl, dangle, float, slip, slide,* and so forth. Have them visualize such descriptions, either by acting them out or by illustrating them.

SECRETS OF THE RAIN FOREST—Nonfiction

During Reading

Independent Reading
For students who are reading independently, you may wish to make a quick check of comprehension at the midpoint and at the end of *Secrets of the Rain Forest*, using these questions.

Midpoint
Comprehension Check
- Why do you think the author refers to many of the animals and plants as "secrets." *(Several have been recently discovered, and there are many yet to be discovered.)* **Critical: Making Judgments**
- Why are the rain forests described as being like the earth's "lungs?" *(Plants take in carbon dioxide and give off oxygen.)* **Critical: Making Comparisons**

End of Book
Comprehension Check
- Why is it important that people begin taking steps to preserve the rain forest? *(If deforestation is allowed to continue at its present rate, the rain forests will eventually be completely destroyed.)* **Critical: Cause and Effect**
- What things are you willing to do to help preserve the rain forest? *(Answers will vary.)* **Creative: Personal Reaction**

Teacher-Supported Reading
For students who are reading with **teacher support**, use the chapter-by-chapter **Comprehension Checks** as a quick check of students' understanding. **Teachable Moments** are referenced to highlight points during reading at which you might wish to use a **Skill Mini-Lesson**. **Reader Response** questions are also provided. From time to time, you may wish to have students respond to these questions in writing.

Chapter 1 (Pages 5–10)

Comprehension Check
- Why are tropical rain forests among the most unique places on the earth? *(More varieties of plants and animals live there than anywhere else on the earth.)* **Critical: Main Idea**
- On which continent do you see the greatest amount of rain forest? *(South America)* **Study Skills: Using Graphic Aids—Maps**

Teachable Moment
As students read the map on pages 8–9, you might wish to use the Study Skills Mini-Lesson: Using Graphic Aids—Maps on page 86.

Reader Response
- Have you read about any of the rain-forest animals mentioned so far? If so, what did you learn? *(Answers will vary.)* **Reading Across Texts: Prior Knowledge**

Chapter 2 (Pages 11–16)

Comprehension Check
- Why are tropical rain forests so important? *(Tropical rain forests are homes for many interdependent ecosystems of plants and animals. The vast number of trees adds to the earth's oxygen.)* **Critical: Main Idea**
- What are oxygen and carbon dioxide? *(They are gases that are found in air.)* **Critical: Specialized Vocabulary**

Teachable Moment
This may be a good time to use the Word Study Skill Mini-Lesson on Specialized Vocabulary, found on page 87 of this Teacher's Guide.

Reader Response
- If you were a scientist studying the rain forest, what would you most like to study? Why? *(Answers will vary.)* **Creative: Personal Reaction**

SECRETS OF THE RAIN FOREST—Nonfiction

SECRETS OF THE RAIN FOREST

Chapter 3 (Pages 17–21)

Comprehension Check
- What did people who came to the rain forest long ago discover? *(Plants and animals that were strange to them. Useful plants such as rubber trees.)* **Critical: Synthesizing Information**
- How was Orellana's trip down the Amazon River different from what he expected? *(He expected to find food quickly and return. He went a long way to find food; the river was too fast to return; he saw a land unlike anything he had seen before.)* **Critical: Drawing Conclusions**
- Why was Theodore Roosevelt's trip to the rain forest important? *(The group he was with brought back many examples of living things that had not been seen before.)* **Critical: Making Inferences**

Reader Response
- Would you like to visit a tropical rain forest? Why or why not? *(Answers will vary.)* **Creative: Personal Reaction**

Chapter 4 (Pages 22–28)

Comprehension Check
- How are the three layers of plant growth in the rain forest similar to a three-story apartment building? *(Different things live at each level of the rain forest just as families live on different levels of an apartment building.)* **Critical: Making Comparisons**
- What are two of the meanings you know for the word *story*? *(A story one reads in a book; a level or floor)* **Critical: Multiple-Meaning Words**

Teachable Moment (Skill Master)
You may wish to use the Word Study Skill Mini-Lesson on Multiple-Meaning Words found on page 87.

Reader Response
- Of the plants described in the book, which would you most like to see in real life? Why? **Creative: Personal Response**

Chapter 5 (Pages 29–36)

Comprehension Check
- Read the chapter title and examine the illustrations in this chapter. Which of the following questions might you expect to be answered in this chapter: What kind of medicines are found in rain-forest plants? Which rain-forest animals live in the trees? Why are rain-forest frogs so colorful? *(Questions 2 and 3 should be answered by this chapter.)* **Study Skills: SQ3R**

Teachable Moment
This would be a good time to use the Study Skills Mini-Lesson: SQ3R on page 86 of this Teacher's Guide.

- Have you ever used camouflage in your own life? If so, how? *(Answers will vary.)* **Critical: Synthesizing Information**

Reader Response
- Which animal of the tropical rain forest do you find most fascinating? Why? *(Answers will vary.)* **Creative: Personal Expression**

Chapter 6 (Pages 37–40)

Comprehension Check
- Why do you think the author wrote Chapter 6 of this book? *(to give readers an introduction to some of the people who make the rain forest their home)* **Critical: Author's Purpose**
- How is the Amazon River important to the people who live along it? *(They eat fish from the river; in their boats, they use the river like a highway.)* **Critical: Main Idea**

Teachable Moment (Skill Master)
You may wish to use the Comprehension Skill Mini-Lesson on Main Idea and Details on page 85 of this Teacher's Guide.

Reader Response
- In what ways are Yanomami get-togethers similar or different from get-togethers you and your family have? *(Answers will vary.)* **Creative: Personal Response**

82 SECRETS OF THE RAIN FOREST—Nonfiction

Chapter 7 (Pages 41–47)

Comprehension Check
- How does the way people around the world spend money affect the rain forest? *(If people are buying non-renewable goods, and goods made from rain-forest animals and plants, they contribute to the destruction of the rain forest.)* **Critical: Drawing Conclusions**

Teachable Moment
You may wish to use the Comprehension Skill Mini-Lesson: Drawing Conclusions, found on page 85, at this time.

- How can people help protect the earth's rain forests? *(Exercise care with the kinds of things they buy; buy renewable goods; save energy; and so on)* **Critical: Main Idea**

Reader Response
- Why do you think it is important to help save the rain forests? *(Answers will vary.)* **Creative: Personal Response**

More English as a Second Language

Students may benefit from looking at the region in which they live through the use of the vocabulary words. For example, the *climate* of the rain forest is described as warm and wet. What is the *climate* of the place where students live? Have them write words and phrases to describe the climate such as warm for part of the year, cold for part of the year, and so on. The rain-forest *ecosystem* consists of huge trees and vines, colorful animals, meat-eating plants, and other unusual organisms. Ask students questions such as: What animals and plants are found in your *ecosystem*? What *poisonous* things can you name? What *crops* are grown nearby?

SECRETS OF THE RAIN FOREST—Nonfiction

After Reading

Reader Response Activities

After students have completed *Secrets of the Rain Forest*, you may wish to choose from the following activities.

Writing a News Article

Ask students to imagine that they were along as some of the early explorers discovered the rain forest. Have them write a news article explaining what was discovered. **Writing**

Giving a Speech

Invite students to prepare a short speech about why it is important to save the rain forest. When they are ready, students can deliver the speech to the class. Class members can then ask questions for the speaker to answer. **Listening/Speaking**

Listening to Rain-Forest Sounds

Bring in a cassette with the sounds of rain-forest animals for students to listen to. Although the recording is likely to identify the sounds, students might also try to match sounds with the animals they have read about in the text. **Listening**

CURRICULUM CONNECTIONS

Geography Activity
Tracing the Amazon River

Have students use a map to trace the Amazon River and some of its larger tributaries. Have them find out where the Amazon begins and ends.

Mathematics Activity
Figuring Out How Much Rain Forest Remains

Using the information on page 42, have students determine how much rain forest remains in Costa Rica. Have them look at the map on the left and compare it to the map on the right side of the page. Then have them determine a fraction based on a visual estimate.

Social Studies Activity
Researching a Rain-Forest People

Invite students to work in pairs or small groups to use an encyclopedia to find out the names of different peoples who live in the rain forest and information about how they live. Have students share their findings with the class.

Science Research Activity
Finding Out More About Rain-Forest Animals

Encourage students to choose an animal from the text and find out more about it. Ask students to answer questions such as: Is the species endangered? Is it a predatory animal? If so, what does it eat? If it is a prey animal, what are its enemies? Where does it fit in the rain-forest food web?

Skill Mini-Lessons

The following skill lessons may be used while or after students read the book *Secrets of the Rain Forest*.

COMPREHENSION: Main Idea And Details

Objective: To identify the main idea and supporting details

Teach
Recall with students that the Yanomami people get their food from the rain forest. Explain that this is a main or important idea about the Yanomami people in Chapter 6. Encourage students to look on page 39 and find details that support this main idea. *(They gather plants like palm fruits, Brazil nuts, and bananas. They hunt animals such as small rodents, lizards, and insects.)*

Practice
On the chalkboard, write *Many rain-forest plants contain substances that can be used to make medicines*. Have students look on page 27 to identify supporting details for this main idea.

Then have students reread page 25. Encourage them to suggest a main idea for the details about the lianas.

Evaluate
You may wish to use Comprehension Skill Master: Main Idea and Details on page 90 to evaluate students' understanding of the skill.

COMPREHENSION: Drawing Conclusions

Objective: To determine ideas or information not directly stated in the text

Teach
Remind students that much of Chapter 7 addresses ways that individuals can help save the rain forest. Point out that although the author never states this directly, they can figure out that the way people spend money affects the rain forest. Have students find examples of information in Chapter 7 that support this conclusion.

Invite students to find examples of information that describe buying patterns that hurt the rain forest, and buying patterns that help the rain forest. For example, is the rain forest helped or harmed by buying rain-forest animals as pets? Is it helped or harmed by buying renewable goods?

Practice
Have students reread the text on page 43. Ask them to choose the sentence below that states a conclusion that can be drawn from this information. Ask them to justify their choice.

- If the rain forests disappear, the animals and people who live there will move someplace else.
- The earth will be a much poorer place without the rain forests.
- If the rain forests are destroyed, they will eventually come back.

Evaluate
Have students practice reading a page or section of the text and drawing a conclusion from the information given.

STUDY SKILLS: Using Graphic Aids—Maps

Objective: To use a map to find specific information

Teach

Have students refer to the map on pages 8–9. Ask them how they figured out which continent has the most rain-forest area. Point out that maps contain a wide variety of information and show this information in a variety of ways. Many maps show continents, oceans, and rivers, as well as countries and cities. Different maps show special information such as the amount of rainfall, crops, natural resources, or historical places. Maps use color, printed labels, and symbols to show different information. Have students describe the legend, and major entries on this map.

Encourage volunteers to locate the following on the map: the Atlantic Ocean, Brazil, the equator, the island of Madagascar.

Ask students how directions—north, south, east, and west, are identified on the map. Then have a volunteer use the compass rose to determine if most of the South American rain forest is north or south of the equator.

Practice

Have students use the map to answer the following questions: Through which continents does the equator run? Which ocean lies to the east of the Amazon rain forest?

Evaluate

Check students' understanding of using maps by asking questions based on the information on the maps on page 42.

STUDY SKILLS: SQ3R

Objective: Use the Survey, Question, Read, Recite, and Review process to address reading material

Teach

Have students recall that in order to study specific reading material, they can apply several steps as they read. First, they can survey a specific portion, such as a chapter. This includes reading the title and examining the illustrations, including reading the captions. From this survey they can write two or three questions that they would expect to be answered by the reading material.

Next, they can read the material silently and also write the answers to the questions they asked. Following silent reading they can recite the text aloud to themselves or take turns reading it aloud with a classmate

or with a group. Finally, they can review the material by looking again at the title, illustrations and captions, questions, answers, and other notes they have taken.

Practice

Have students apply SQ3R to Chapter 3 by surveying the title, pictures, and captions, asking questions based on their survey, applying a silent reading and reciting aloud strategy as they read the text, and then reviewing what they have read.

Evaluate

Have volunteers describe their SQ3R results from the Practice exercise, in order to check students' understanding of the study process.

WORD STUDY: Specialized Vocabulary

Objective: To understand that specific content areas have specialized vocabulary and that readers must often use context to determine word meaning

Teach

Remind students of the question in Chapter 2 about the meaning of *oxygen* and *carbon dioxide*. They were able to determine that these two things are gases because they are part of air, and students know that the air is made of gases. Tell students that specialized vocabulary is found in material about many subjects, such as computers, sports, or science. Sometimes a new vocabulary word is defined in the text. But often a reader has to use the context to figure out what it means.

Have students consider the word *atmosphere* on page 15. Read aloud the first two sentences on the page. Have students note that the word *atmosphere* in the second sentence is not defined. But it is used as a synonym for the word *air* in the first sentence. This is one way of using context to figure out the meaning.

Practice

Have students reread pages 8, 11, and 12 that contain the specialized vocabulary words *ecosystem, climate,* and *species.* In each case, have students determine word meaning and tell whether they learned this through definition or context.

Evaluate

Stop and check occasionally during read-aloud sessions to focus on specialized vocabulary words. Be sure students can find the meanings, either by direct definition or through context.

WORD STUDY: Multiple-Meaning Words

Objective: To understand that some words have more than one meaning and that meaning can be determined by context

Teach

Write the following on the chalkboard:

The *plant* withered in the hot sun.
Dad *will* work at the *plant* this weekend.

Tell students that there are two meanings of the word *plant* used in the sentences. One meaning is "building used for a manufacturing process." The other meaning is "a living thing with leaves, roots, and a soft stem." Ask the class which meaning of the word *plant* is used in each sentence. How do they know? *(the way the word is used in each sentence)* Explain that readers must figure out the context—the way the word is used—to determine which meaning of a multiple-meaning word is used.

Practice

Ask students to determine the meaning of the underlined word in each sentence.

1. Tropical rain forests are found along a narrow <u>band</u> near the equator.
2. The <u>band</u> played a marching song.
3. Some species don't survive a <u>change</u> of climate.
4. She counted the <u>change</u> very carefully.

Evaluate

You may wish to use Word Study Skill Master: Multiple-Meaning Words to evaluate students' understanding of the skill.

SECRETS OF THE RAIN FOREST—Nonfiction

Home-School Connection

Dear Family,

Our class is reading chapter books that have to do with discoveries. The book we are reading is *Secrets of the Rain Forest* by Edward Myers. It tells about the plants, animals, people, and overall importance of the earth's tropical rain forests.

Discover Together

- You may want to go to the local library to help your child find out more about rain forests. Here are some books to look for:

    Rain Forest Secrets by Arthur Doros (Scholastic 1990)

    What's in the Rain Forest? by Suzanne Ross (Enchanted Rain Forest Press, 1991)

- Check your local video store for documentaries or movies about rain forests such as *Ferngully* and *Ferngully 2*.
- Visit a rain-forest exhibit in a local natural history museum or other organization with traveling or permanent displays.

Conexión con el hogar

Estimada familia:

En este capítulo, nuestra clase está leyendo libros que están relacionados con descubrimientos. El libro que estamos leyendo en la actualidad se titula *Secrets of the Rain Forest* de Edward Myers, que trata sobre las plantas, los animales, la gente y la importancia general de los bosques tropicales en la Tierra.

Descubran juntos

- Pueden visitar la biblioteca local para ayudar a su hijo/a a aprender más acerca de los bosques tropicales. Estos son algunos de los libros que pueden buscar:

    Rain Forest Secrets de Arthur Doros (Scholastic, 1990)

    What's in the Rain Forest? de Suzanne Ross (Enchanted Rain Forest Press, 1991)

- Busquen en la tienda de vídeos local documentales o películas acerca de bosques tropicales tales como *Ferngully* y *Ferngully 2*.
- Visiten una exhibición sobre bosques tropicales en un museo de historia natural local u otra organización con exposiciones temporales o permanentes.

VOCABULARY MASTER

Name _____

Vocabulary: Glossary Words

Fill each each blank with a vocabulary word from the box.

| climate | pollute | renewable | camouflage | deforestation |
| recent | recycle | atmosphere | poisonous | ecosystem |

The rain forest is full of animals and plants. It is a wonderful (1) _____. On a (2) _____ trip we went to a rain forest. We had to get used to the hot and humid (3) _____. The guide took us to see farmers who were growing rubber trees. Some people were burning the forests. Smoke drifted into the (4) _____ and started to (5) _____ the air. The (6) _____ left many hillsides bare of trees.

We loved seeing the colorful tree frogs. They do not need (7) _____. Other animals stay away from these frogs because they are very (8) _____. I am going to (9) _____ my newspapers and cans to help save the rain forests. I am also going to use products that are (10) _____.

SECRETS OF THE RAIN FOREST—Nonfiction

SKILL MASTER

Name _____

Comprehension: Main Idea and Details

A main idea is an important idea. It tells what a paragraph or page is mainly about. Supporting details tell more about the main idea.

Read the main idea in the box. Look in *Secrets of the Rain Forest* and find details that support this main idea. Write the details on the lines. Then draw a picture that tells about the main idea.

> **Main Idea:** Camouflaged animals hide by blending into the rain forest.

1. _____
2. _____
3. _____

Name _____

Word Study: Multiple-Meaning Words

Read the definitions for each multiple-meaning word in the box. Then read the sentences. In each blank, write the letter of the definition that tells how the underlined word is used in the sentence.

> (A) **coast**—land along an ocean or sea
>
> (B) **coast**—to ride or slide without much effort
>
> (C) **light**—form of energy that lets us see
>
> (D) **light**—not heavy, without much weight
>
> (E) **current**—a flow of electricity through a wire
>
> (F) **current**—a flow of water in a river or ocean
>
> (G) **current**—regarding the present time

1. The canoe was light, and we carried it for miles. _____

2. Is that newspaper current? _____

3. We liked to coast down the hill on our sled. _____

4. The current went off, and so did our power. _____

5. The river's current got faster near the falls. _____

6. The explorers sailed along the coast and saw the Amazon. _____

7. Little light from the sun reached the forest floor. _____

GRAPHIC ORGANIZER

Name _____

Fix-Up Strategies

What do you know after reading the text the first time?	What more do you know after rereading the text at a slower rate?

How does rereading at a slower pace help you understand what you read?

GRAPHIC ORGANIZER

Name _____

Visualizing—Plot

This story begins when _____
_____
_____
_____

A problem the characters have is _____
_____
_____
_____
_____

They try to solve the problem by _____
_____
_____
_____
_____
_____

They finally solve the problem when _____
_____
_____
_____
_____
_____

GRAPHIC ORGANIZER

Name _____

Self-Assess

What did you learn?	What was the best part?
What questions do you still have?	What could you do to answer your questions?

Set 4 DISCOVERIES

GRAPHIC ORGANIZER

Name _____

Character Map

What can you tell about characters from the way they act? Choose four characters and write your opinions about them in the picture frames.

Character:

Character:

Character:

Character:

Set 4 DISCOVERIES

GRAPHIC ORGANIZER

Name _____

Synthesize Information

Topic:

What do you know?

How do you know?

What new ideas do you have?

Set 4 DISCOVERIES